# More endorsements for
## *Early Childhood Education for a New Era*

"Goffin is comfortable with being provocative. She invites us to a challenging and perhaps difficult conversation. As you read, you can feel her passion and respect for the field and its history. You can also sense the urgency. We need to begin these fieldwide discussions. It's time."
—Deb Flis, director, Connecticut Accreditation Facilitation Project, Connecticut Charts a Course

"Vintage Goffin. She pulls no punches and reminds us that the time is right for coming together to exert leadership. Few of our leaders are as well versed and prepared with the knowledge, passion, and maturity to offer a visionary plan of action to achieve the status of a profession."
—Josué Cruz, former president, National Association for the Education of Young Children

"Goffin's look at the ECE field presents important and challenging questions to everyone working within and around ECE. All ECE policymakers should read it. *ECE for a New Era* disrupts many of the narratives we adopt about this work and forces us to examine the space we inhabit in a field that, while undefined, is rapidly changing."
—Don Titcombe, manager, Texas Early Learning Council

"Goffin's review of what she labels a 'defining moment' for the care and education of young children in our country is indeed provocative. She convincingly argues that the time has come for all of us involved in this complex field to resolve those issues crucial to the future of early childhood education."
—Lilian G. Katz, professor emerita, Early Childhood and Parenting Collaborative, University of Illinois

# EARLY CHILDHOOD EDUCATION SERIES

Sharon Ryan, *Editor*

Early Childhood Education for a New Era:
Leading for Our Profession
STACIE G. GOFFIN

Everyday Artists: Inquiry and Creativity in the
Early Childhood Classroom
DANA FRANTZ BENTLEY

Multicultural Teaching in the Early Childhood
Classroom: Approaches, Strategies, and Tools,
Preschool–2nd Grade
MARIANA SOUTO-MANNING

Inclusion in the Early Childhood Classroom:
What Makes a Difference?
SUSAN L. RECCHIA & YOON-JOO LEE

Language Building Blocks:
Essential Linguistics for Early Childhood Educators
ANITA PANDEY

Understanding the Language Development and Early
Education of Hispanic Children.
EUGENE E. GARCÍA & ERMINDA H. GARCÍA

Moral Classrooms, Moral Children: Creating a
Constructivist Atmosphere in Early Education, 2nd Ed.
RHETA DeVRIES & BETTY ZAN

Defending Childhood:
Keeping the Promise of Early Education
BEVERLY FALK, ED.

Don't Leave the Story in the Book: Using Literature to
Guide Inquiry in Early Childhood Classrooms
MARY HYNES-BERRY

Starting with Their Strengths: Using the Project
Approach in Early Childhood Special Education
DEBORAH C. LICKEY & DENISE J. POWERS

The Play's the Thing:
Teachers' Roles in Children's Play, 2nd Ed.
ELIZABETH JONES & GRETCHEN REYNOLDS

Twelve Best Practices for Early Childhood Education:
Integrating Reggio and Other Inspired Approaches
ANN LEWIN-BENHAM

Big Science for Growing Minds:
Constructivist Classrooms for Young Thinkers
JACQUELINE GRENNON BROOKS

What If All the Kids Are White? Anti-Bias Multicultural
Education with Young Children and Families, 2nd Ed.
LOUISE DERMAN-SPARKS & PATRICIA G. RAMSEY

Seen and Heard:
Children's Rights in Early Childhood Education
ELLEN LYNN HALL & JENNIFER KOFKIN RUDKIN

Young Investigators: The Project Approach in the
Early Years, 2nd Ed.
JUDY HARRIS HELM & LILIAN G. KATZ

Supporting Boys' Learning: Strategies for Teacher
Practice, PreK–Grade 3
BARBARA SPRUNG, MERLE FROSCHL, & NANCY GROPPER

Young English Language Learners: Current Research
and Emerging Directions for Practice and Policy
EUGENE E. GARCÍA & ELLEN C. FREDE, EDS.

Connecting Emergent Curriculum and Standards
in the Early Childhood Classroom: Strengthening
Content and Teacher Practice
SYDNEY L. SCHWARTZ & SHERRY M. COPELAND

Infants and Toddlers at Work: Using Reggio-Inspired
Materials to Support Brain Development
ANN LEWIN-BENHAM

The View from the Little Chair in the Corner:
Improving Teacher Practice and Early Childhood
Learning (Wisdom from an Experienced Classroom
Observer)
CINDY RZASA BESS

Culture and Child Development in Early Childhood
Programs: Practices for Quality Education and Care
CAROLLEE HOWES

The Early Intervention Guidebook for Families and
Professionals: Partnering for Success
BONNIE KEILTY

The Story in the Picture:
Inquiry and Artmaking with Young Children
CHRISTINE MULCAHEY

Educating and Caring for Very Young Children:
The Infant/Toddler Curriculum, 2nd Ed.
DORIS BERGEN, REBECCA REID, & LOUIS TORELLI

Beginning School:
U.S. Policies in International Perspective
RICHARD M. CLIFFORD & GISELE M. CRAWFORD, EDS.

Emergent Curriculum in the Primary Classroom:
Interpreting the Reggio Emilia Approach in Schools
CAROL ANNE WIEN, ED.

---

For a list of other titles in this series, visit www.tcpress.com

*(continued)*

# Early Childhood Education for a New Era

## Leading for Our Profession

### Stacie G. Goffin

*Foreword by Mary Jean Schumann,*
*DNP, MBA, RN, CPNP, FAAN*

Teachers College, Columbia University
New York and London

Published by Teachers College Press, 1234 Amsterdam Avenue, New York, NY 10027

Copyright © 2013 by Teachers College, Columbia University

*Library of Congress Cataloging-in-Publication Data can be found at www.loc.gov.*

ISBN 978-0-8077-5460-3 (paper)
ISBN 978-0-8077-5461-0 (hardcover)
ISBN 978-0-8077-7260-7 (ebook)

Printed on acid-free paper
Manufactured in the United States of America

20   19   18   17   16   15   14   13          8   7   6   5   4   3   2   1

*To Bruce*

# Contents

# Foreword

Some books primarily inform; this one does much more. *Early Childhood Education for a New Era: Leading for Our Profession* shares the history of early childhood education (ECE) and makes the case for organizing the field as a profession. Along the way it surfaces a moral imperative: ECE's responsibility to children. After reading the book I concluded early childhood educators are letting society down by not advancing the field's collective competence to serve all children well.

I have been a master's prepared pediatric nurse for nearly 40 years, a board certified pediatric nurse practitioner for 30 of them, and for 20 of these years a national nurse leader. Even so, when I was a family child care provider early in my career, I grappled with how to meet children's developmental and emotional needs. Parents, regardless of economic and educational status, depend on others to focus daily attention on their child's developmental needs and achievements, which is why I'm pleased to write this foreword on behalf of professionalizing ECE.

Many parallels exist between the profession of nursing and ECE. Core to both are societal obligations to protect the public's welfare. Nurses improve and promote health and well-being; they ease pain, suffering, and loss. ECE protects, supports, and educates children and by extension, engages and supports parents, modeling ways to protect and encourage children's development.

Nursing came together as a field of practice not only to meet the needs of individuals receiving care, but also to establish consistent standards that would elevate our social standing and protect society from those who were incompetent or ill-intentioned. In the nearly 120 years since nursing sought professional recognition, we have steadfastly resisted intrusion by other disciplines or policymakers attempting to dictate or regulate nursing standards or scopes of practice, even as we have collaborated with medicine and other disciplines to increase the knowledge base of our professionals.

Nursing has assumed accountability for its practice and for addressing issues that threaten its capacity to carry out its mission. Its contract with society demands that we meet societal gaps in care, provide increasingly more educated and competent practitioners, and protect society from imposters. Nursing's evolution, not only as a profession but also as a driver for change within and outside of the profession, offers ECE four lessons as it addresses its moral imperative.

**1. Identify a unique body of knowledge that is known and practiced by every member of the profession.** Critical to establishing and surviving as a profession is basing one's practice on a specialized body of knowledge that is not "known" by everyone. Because others less well educated and parents and family members believe they perform work similar to early childhood educators, the discipline must chart the whole breadth and depth of its core knowledge so its domain of specialized expertise is well articulated. Otherwise detractors can discount its societal value and importance. Nursing is familiar with this challenge. It repeatedly experiences medicine's attempts to control nursing's "domain" and short-sell nursing by offering cheaper substitutes such as medical assistants.

Based on the history shared in *ECE for a New Era*, identification of the field's domain-specific knowledge is largely being driven by policymakers and external funders, rather than by the ECE field. Drawing from nursing's experiences, ECE needs to step up and take charge of defining and determining education and performance expectations for its practitioners so children can be beneficiaries of its expertise.

**2. Identify and stay focused on the field's core work.** While advocacy is a critical component at every level of nursing practice, nurses are expected to demonstrate competence through application of the profession's core knowledge, that is, provide high-quality, safe care that returns individuals to health and maintains or improves the health of individuals and populations. Even while advocating for the needs of children, ECE leadership's first priority has to be the core work of promoting each child's greatest potential in terms of growth and development. To move forward as a recognized profession, ECE's core "business" must be identified and supported through an inclusive consensus building process, even if it means every stakeholder organization must give up something for the goal to be achieved.

**3. Champion fieldwide leadership by identifying or creating an overarching umbrella organization that facilitates inclusive consensus building.** When someone has asked who decides how ECE moves forward as a field of practice, the answer has been, "I don't know" (this volume). Fragmentation poses challenges for nursing, too. We have over a hundred national organizations representing various specialties and ethnically diverse groups of nurses. Still, large or small, all operate, noisily and imperfectly at times, under the larger umbrella of nursing.

Despite its diversity and because of its ethical obligations to serve, nursing uses large scale consensus processes under the aegis of one or more of its professional associations to define scopes and standards of practice for the registered nurse (RN) as well as for advanced practice nurses and a host of specialty practice areas. Such consensus, ever dynamic, provides the foundation for accreditation of education programs, individual licensure, and practice recognition such as certification.

***4. Prepare every new and existing member of the profession to lead.*** Leadership and professionalism is the obligation of every member of a profession. Every student as well as every direct care nurse, supervisor, manager, nurse educator, and nurse executive have a role as a professional leader. Nursing has found that consistently focusing on leadership skills is critical to the profession's advancement on behalf of those it serves.

One of the missteps nursing made 40 years ago was evolving to include three entry routes into the profession as registered nurses. RNs can gain entry and licensure through an associate degree, baccalaureate degree, or even as a non-degreed nurse through a few dozen remaining diploma programs. Each route provides eligibility to take the same licensure exam. This has created decades of confusion for consumers and colleagues about the level of knowledge and skills RNs possess. Many non-baccalaureate programs place more emphasis on technical skills and less emphasis on critical thinking, nursing leadership, and professional behavior. Politicians and others gain an avenue for addressing nursing shortages through shortsighted quick fixes such as expansion of associate degree programs that limit professional advancement and dilute the pool of leadership talent.

After more than 40 years, nursing recently committed to attaining by 2020 the minimum of baccalaureate nursing education for 80% of its RN work force. The lesson here is to avoid compromising ECE academic educational preparation and progression once the field's core knowledge is determined and to teach and reinforce professional leadership at every step.

Achieving professional recognition required decades of effort by nurses who labored to establish the field's standards and scopes of practice, identified the profession's unique body of knowledge and then built upon it, and assumed accountability for its members' competence. As a profession nursing has and will continue to struggle with policymakers and other disciplines over what constitutes nursing practice. But as a result of decades of work, there is never doubt that we will advocate proactively for improvements in quality based on our specialized knowledge base. From society's perspective, ECE should begin forming itself as a profession so it can do the same.

–Mary Jean Schumann, DNP, MBA, RN, CPNP, FAAN

# Acknowledgments

When this journey began, my intent was to examine the field's leadership approach to effecting change between 1950 and 2000 as a segue to highlighting the dramatically changed context for early childhood education in the 21st century and the need for new and different forms of leadership. To anchor this examination, three exemplary and distinctive leaders were identified–Barbara Bowman, Lilian Katz, and Gwen Morgan–each of whom shaped early childhood education during the latter half of the twentieth century. Their influence extends to state and national policy and practice across every sector of early childhood education: child care, Head Start, Pre-Kindergarten, Kindergarten, and every facet of the field's efforts to improve early learning experiences for young children. Issues they championed were to help document shifts in the field's context and changes in its leadership needs.

Limitations to this reasoning ultimately led to my dismissing this approach. Yet Barbara, Lilian, and Gwen graciously continued to support my writing efforts through conversations, emails, and their extensive portfolio of publications, transitioning in function from "leadership anchors" to "leadership mentors." I owe deep gratitude to each of them.

Writing *Early Childhood Education for a New Era: Leading for Our Profession* led to my initiating two novel studies to assist with questions lacking answers from existing research: one a study of fieldwide leadership (Goffin, 2009) and the second an exploration of ECE leadership development programs (Goffin & Means, 2009). Much appreciated funding support from the McCormick Foundation made these two studies possible.

Innumerable colleagues–you know who you are–and participants at presentations and keynote addresses listened to my evolving thinking, questioned, challenged, and encouraged me to "stick with it." Still other colleagues, including Brenda Boyd, Millie Cowles, Harriet Egertson, Stephanie Feeney, and Deb Flis, read various versions of the manuscript, sometimes more than once, and offered insightful comments and encouragement. Marie Ellen Larcada, at Teachers College Press, and Sharon Ryan, editor of the Early Childhood Education Series, patiently waited for the manuscript; their continuing belief in what I was trying to accomplish was always uplifting. To my editors, thank you for improving the book's clarity and presentation.

And now I turn to those who engaged with me in preparing the book's final iteration. In this regard, special appreciation goes to Mary Jean Schumann, interim senior associate dean of the George Washington University's School of Nursing, who authored the Foreword. Mary Jean and I met when I was researching examples of fieldwide leadership. Our relationship evolved from a "cold call" to one of innumerable lunch discussions about professions and their challenges. Rolf Grafwallner, Assistant State Superintendent of Maryland's Division of Early Childhood Development in the Department of Education; Jacqueline Jones, former Deputy Assistant Secretary for Policy and Early Learning in the U.S. Department of Education; and Pam Winton, Director of Outreach and Senior Researcher at the FPG Child Development Institute, wrote the Next Steps Commentaries. Their commentaries highlight not only the opportunity for challenging and exciting conversations going forward but also concretely convey that next steps are available to us. The bios of these four dynamic individuals reveal the depth of expertise and experience they brought to their task. I am indebted to each of these four colleagues for their willingness to be a part of this venture and to join with me in prodding early childhood education to consider its obligations to children and families. My appreciation also goes to the authors of the book's endorsements, still further indication of the timeliness of the book's ideas.

To each and all of you: Thank you for your friendship, support, and tremendous work on behalf of competent practice by early childhood education practitioners.

Finally, I am surrounded by strong and nurturing family members: Sabra and Dave, whose encouragement is ever present—and we all enthusiastically welcome Maya Isabel, who was born this past February. *Early Childhood Education for a New Era* is dedicated to my husband, Bruce. To know him is to understand the depth of love and support he brings into my life.

# Preface

"Where is early childhood education going?" As I thought about what to say to this question, a whole lot more questions popped up. For example:

1. Where are we now?
2. And where have we been?
3. And where are we going if we continue to do what we are doing now?
4. And what should we be doing if we want to go somewhere else?
5. Where else would that be?
6. And where do we want early childhood education to go?
7. And where do we hope it is not going? (Katz, 2007)

Given the upheavals early childhood education (ECE) has experienced during 200 plus years of history, field-altering change is not an anomaly. *Early Childhood Education for a New Era: Leading for Our Profession* voices this refrain yet one more time by identifying the present as a *defining* moment in ECE's evolution as a field of practice. It offers a framework for responding to Katz's challenging questions and urges ECE as a field of practice to assume responsibility for the answers. In contrast to those whose solutions routinely target state and federal policy, it points to ECE as the agent for change.

Writing *Ready or Not: Leadership Choices in Early Care and Education* (Goffin & Washington, 2007) coalesced my thinking on core leadership and development challenges facing ECE: defining the field's core purpose, forming its social identity, and committing to shared obligations to children and families. I still wrestled, though, with why, after the auspicious onset of ECE during the mid-1800s to early 1900s, it remains a field still divided by its multi-rooted history.

## DEFINING TERMS

In searching for an answer, *Early Childhood Education for a New Era: Leading for Our Profession* (*ECE for a New Era*) goes beyond formative ideas presented in *Ready or Not*. It examines the field's history to understand why ECE remains divided as a *field of practice* and presses the urgency of creating an alternative trajectory for the future. This includes basics such as uniting around the field's name and identifying what is encompassed by the term *early childhood education.*

As a writer, knowing what term to use is always challenging given the array of options and their political nuances. I've chosen *early childhood education.* Previously, I have relied on *early care and education,* viewing it as a term fostering cohesion among the field's many subdivisions. In writing *ECE for a New Era,* however, I came to value a term capable of succinctly stating the field's purpose. *Early childhood education* fulfills this objective, encompassing the field's multiple sectors and commitments to early learning, responsive and caring relationships, and early development.

In terms of the field's chronological span, answers most often are associated with early learning systems (which establish a border for ECE as a system of programs, services, and policies) serving children birth through age 8, birth to age 5, or birth to the start of Kindergarten. *ECE for a New Era* aligns with the border definitions offered by Kagan and Kauerz (2012). They define an *early care and education system* as one including programs explicitly addressing the early care and education needs of young children from birth to age 5, encompassing the full range of ECE settings that children encounter prior to Kindergarten.

A broader term, *early learning system,* includes the programs and services of an early care and education system plus Kindergarten through 3rd grade, thereby inclusively addressing children's education from birth through age 8. While acknowledging the importance of comprehensive services such as health and mental health, these two definitions place these services outside the early care and education and early learning systems (Kagan & Kauerz, 2012, p. 9).

## HOW THE BOOK IS ORGANIZED

*ECE for a New Era* argues for organizing ECE as a professional field of practice, which, to be achieved, will require leadership from all of us. "To lead," according to Kahane (2010), means "to step forward, to exceed one's authority, to try to change the status quo, to exercise power [meaning drive to achieve one's purpose], and such action is by definition disruptive" (p. 116).

This book presses the field to step forward, risk being disruptive, and engage with the emotionally and intellectually challenging work of re-forming ECE as a field of practice. Chapter 1 begins by reminding readers why the time has come to call the question of "What defines and bounds ECE as a field of practice?" (Goffin & Washington, 2007), and makes a case for unifying ECE as a professional field of practice. Building on this foundation, Chapter 2 offers a new lens for understanding the field's present status and assesses current field-unifying strategies. Chapters 3 and 4 examine issues associated with forming ECE as an organized field of practice. The final chapter offers next steps, focusing on what's needed to step forward: altering our individual frames of reference so openness exists for moving forward together as field of practice; recognizing systemic attitudes and behaviors; convening a microcosm of the field to explore next steps; and building capacity through individual and fieldwide leadership. Each chapter builds on the ones that precede it. The book concludes with three individually authored Next Steps Commentaries suggesting concrete steps for transforming ECE into a professional field of practice.

*ECE for a New Era* is written for those who want to improve ECE's collective competence as a field of practice. It should be of particular interest to those of us ready to come together to rethink the field's present trajectory. Many others will be needed to inform and support ECE's development as a profession, but it starts with us.

While allied with the field's historic self-designation as a profession, a structure for ECE as a 21st-century profession is left open-ended. Two intertwined rationales justify this tactic: First, the field's issues defy easy or pre-conceived answers. A plan for forming ECE as a 21st-century profession must rest on fieldwide dialogue and purposeful decision making. Second, and of equal importance, the work ahead has the highest probability of implementation and sustainability if those of us contributing to, as well as being defined by, the field's unfulfilled potential join together to transform ECE as a field of practice.

Yet since *Ready or Not* was published in 2007, it has become evident that additional scaffolding is needed to advance a fieldwide conversation. *ECE for a New Era* attempts to propel forward movement by identifying habits of mind thwarting ECE's unification as a competent field of practice and drawing attention to the unifying potential of ECE as a professional field of practice.

# WHY I WROTE THIS BOOK

*ECE for a New Era* confronts the disparity between the field's potential contributions to children's learning and development and its occupational competence to achieve them. It burrows under the identity and leadership question of "What defines and bounds early care and education as a field of practice?" to better understand why this question still lingers. It elevates as an obligation the field's need to change its collective performance and lifts up the transformational opportunity provided by organizing ECE as a professional field of practice.

In the process, it distinguishes between child development as a political construct and ECE as a discipline of practice. It discriminates between advocacy efforts targeting expanded public responsibility for children and families' well-being and the *internal advocacy* needed to mobilize changes in the field's structure and leadership capacity so pedagogical, developmental, and content knowledge essential to effective ECE infuses practice and is consistently available to children and their families, regardless of program setting.

While we can look to other fields of practice to help us in this journey (Goffin, 2009; IOM & NRC, 2012; Rhodes & Huston, 2012), it is uncharted territory for ECE. Innumerable acts of initiative, commitment, daring, and persistence will be needed to move the ECE field closer to aspirations that have always inspired the zeal of those of us who care about the present and future of children.

The alternative, of course, is to continue accommodating the status quo, thereby marginalizing ECE's impact as a field of practice. *ECE for a New Era* is written in hopes of combatting this possibility and sparking the dialogue and discussion, decision making, and action that can result in a more deserving future.

# CHAPTER 1

# Calling the Question

Why has ECE not come together around shared purpose and agreed upon responsibilities? In a quest to answer this question, I sought to understand why ECE has sustained its divided personality by examining other fields of practice, especially nursing; probing the field's history; reading accounts of policy developments shaping ECE; and delving into the literature on leadership, systems thinking, and capacity development.

It's time to move beyond unevenly applied improvement strategies and take a stand on the field's obligation to elevate ECE's quality across early learning and development settings—not as a voluntary option but as a pre-requisite for early educators' interactions with children and families. ECE needs to put a stake in the ground, move beyond rhetorical claims to professionalism, and improve collective performance by formally organizing as a professional field of practice.

Given the frequency with which ECE describes itself as a profession, this assertion may not seem groundbreaking. Yet shifting from a loosely connected group of individuals to an organized field of professional practice would be transformational in its implications.

Professions are comprised of individuals with effective command over a defined body of knowledge and skill, requiring verification of the right to practice. Becoming a profession would rewire ECE as a field of practice. It would represent a decisive break with the field's past by transferring to ECE the opportunity and obligation of developing and strengthening individual *and* collective competence. It would attend to systematizing ECE, with a focus on teaching as the field's core work.

In the absence of taking action to organize ECE as a profession and acquiring leadership to orchestrate fieldwide change, ECE will continually subject itself to the fluctuations of social and economic change and suffer the whiplash of political shifts associated with policy formation (see Bellm & Whitebook, 2006; Cohen, 2001; Fuller & Holloway, 1996; Klein, 1992; Morgan, 2001, 2005; Rose, 2010; Zigler, Marsland, & Lord, 2009). It will persist as a disorganized field characterized by irregular practice, under-appreciated practitioners, and escalating intervention from external forces. It will continue to lack a rudder for setting direction when circumstances call for adaptation and a helm for steering the field toward opportunities that can improve its contributions to children's early learning and development.

## A DEFINING MOMENT FOR ECE

ECE has largely evaded the task of defining itself as a field of practice and identifying its responsibility for practitioner competence. Intensified by the field's structural and policy disorganization, erratic public support, and rapid expansion since the 1960s, meekness as a field of practice has contributed to uneven levels of teacher competence and program quality, and an overly complex delivery system. It also has generated a vacuum that is being filled by others who, no longer willing to exercise patience and wait for the field to act, determinedly are securing footholds that will steer the field's future (Goffin & Washington, 2007).

These realities make this moment in time a defining one for ECE. The field's custody of the steps necessary to convert its passion for children's early learning and development into competent, goal-directed practice is at stake. Yet absence of fieldwide leadership leaves ECE without an infrastructure for responding to changing expectations for its work and unprepared to assume a persuasive role in forging its future. (See Definition and Characteristics of Fieldwide Leadership box.)

Not all of the field's challenges can be attributed to external conditions. ECE also has contributed to its present circumstances. Other fields have successfully increased individual competence, improved the overall quality of their field's performance, and elevated the public respect accorded to their work (Goffin, 2009). So could ECE.

## IN EVERY CHALLENGE LIES AN OPPORTUNITY

According to Kahane (2010), who facilitates multifaceted social change initiatives, three types of complexity characterize tough challenges:

1.  When a challenge is *dynamically complex,* cause and effect are interdependent and far apart in time and space. Consequently, a piece-by-piece approach can't succeed. The system, however fragmented or incomplete, has to be contemplated as a whole.

## Definition and Characteristics of Fieldwide Leadership

*Fieldwide leadership* is internally oriented leadership directed at effecting change within a field of practice. It is defined by four characteristics:

- Inwardly focused on a field's need to change.
- Directed toward reforming/transforming a field of practice.
- Focused on moving a field forward as a more viable, coherent, accountable, and respected field of practice.
- Typically systemic, adaptive and/or transformational in nature (Goffin, 2009, p. 2).

A *field* is an invisible world filled with mediums of connections: an invisible structure that connects (Wheatley, 1992.) A field's work is about collective–versus individual–action and responsibility (Dreeben, 2005), which is a central orientation of fieldwide leadership. The term *field of practice* makes clear that the purpose of the field in question revolves around performance of a specialized and shared competence.

2. When *socially complex*, those involved bring different perspectives and interests. As a result, outside experts or authorities cannot resolve the challenge. Rather, those involved must be engaged with its resolution.
3. When *generatively complex*, the future is fundamentally unfamiliar and undetermined. "Best practices," therefore, do not provide solutions. Instead, new "next practice" solutions must be created (p. 5).

These descriptors readily apply to ECE. The field has been the recipient of piecemeal solutions throughout its history, prompting attempts to remedy the resulting patchwork of programs, policies, regulations, practices, and expectations. Further, few would deny the field's social complexity. Its diverse and often divisive perspectives and interests are legendary (Goffin & Washington, 2007). And while seeds outlining the field's future have been sowed, the future has yet to be determined.

ECE clearly is in the midst of a tough challenge. Yet if it chooses, it can become the architect for a future as a respected, professional field of practice–respect earned by competently fostering children's early learning and development. But this will require closing the gap between expressed values, public expectations, and the field's competence (Goffin & Washington, 2007; Heifetz, Grashow, & Linsky, 2009; Senge et al., 2010).

Assuming a leadership role in cultivating the field's future, therefore, requires ECE to not only step up to the opportunity, but also to accept the responsibilities that accompany it. The transformation has to be owned by those of us being asked to change (Heifetz, Grashow, & Linsky, 2009; Kahane, 2012; Kegan & Lahey, 2001; Senge et al., 2010). If it were otherwise, ECE would be at a different place as a field of practice.

## WHY THE TIME IS NOW

ECE's history is marked by episodic additions of new programs (e.g., Kindergarten in the late 1800s; day nurseries/child care in the early 1900s; nursery schools in the 1920s; Head Start in the 1960s; early intervention programs in the 1970s; and Pre-Kindergarten in the 1980s/1990s), each emerging from diverse "statements of need" supported by different funding streams. Until the 1990s, though, this progression generated limited public or political interest. Notwithstanding the political upheavals over creating federal child care standards in the 1970s and confirming Head Start's efficacy in the 1980s, until the 1990s, ECE remained relatively invisible and apolitical as a field of practice—but this no longer is the case.

Between 1950 and 1990, as more women used child care in conjunction with their entrance into the paid labor force and the federal government began financing early intervention programs such as Head Start and early childhood special education, ECE experienced escalating growth. During the 1990s, the first national education goal of "All children in America will start school ready to learn," well-publicized findings on early brain development, economic and cost-benefit analyses, and program evaluation results catapulted ECE to a level of visibility more commensurate with its size and potential.

Masterful marketing and intensified advocacy followed, yielding increased political interest marked by the influx of federal dollars, new state and philanthropic resources, and a shift in public perception from "early care" to "early education."

Kagan and Kauerz (2007) highlight the "educationalizing" of ECE as a significant factor in the field's evolution. Largely driven by the accountability movement in public education, ECE has been compelled to develop content standards, identify child outcomes, assess children's learning, and address alignment with K–12 standards. According to Kagan and Kauerz, "In early childhood education, goals and standards shift the starting point of educational pedagogy from the child to the content.

Although they alter the basic starting point and the fundamental premise of the centrality of the individual child, early learning standards are taking root, shifting a century-old way of thinking about how young children should be educated" (p. 21).

Fostered by communications specialists, this shift helped create a policy-friendly framework for expanding Pre-Kindergarten (Pre-K), a supportive context largely eluding child care (Fuller & Holloway, 1996; Rose, 2010; Zigler, Marsland, & Lord, 2009), further contributing to the field's fractured state. Newfound attention also aroused heightened scrutiny, catalyzing appeals for consistent quality across program settings, equitable access, and demands for accountability that reached a crescendo after the start of the current century.

This changing context, in turn, provided impetus, beginning in the 1990s, for thinking beyond discrete programs and contemplating a more systemic approach to delivering ECE. The field's thought leaders and allies transitioned from programmatic additions to systems building.

These systems building activities home in on the field's disjointed delivery system and fragmented federal and state policies, all of which increase ECE's complexity as a field of practice. Add to this scenario reverberations from the Race to the Top–Early Learning Challenge (2011). By formally encouraging a 50-state approach to systems building and awarding large grants to select states, differences among states likely will widen.

The field's complexity underscores the need for a common denominator capable of addressing variations across programs as well as those existing within and across states. Structuring ECE as a professional field of practice responds to this challenge by attending to the competence of individual practitioners regardless of sponsorship or funding distinctions between program settings.

ECE is being transformed. Almost every facet of the field's work is experiencing change. Lifting from a magazine advertisement for BNY Mellon Wealth Management, "Staying the course is like navigating a new world with an old map."

## WANTED: LEADERSHIP

Admittedly, stepping up to the challenge and opportunity outlined by *ECE for a New Era* will be hard. Responding to the dramatic changes under way and planning for a desired future require not only engaging in the work of finding viable solutions but also in making adaptations that solution(s) will necessitate.

Losses resulting from choosing among cherished values and behaviors are inevitable (Heifetz, 1994; Heifetz, Grashow, & Linsky, 2009). By way of example: Should ECE rely on others to address safety issues generated by the absence of an evenly prepared workforce? Should individuals unprepared for a formal teaching role teach generations of children even if they are taking coursework? What is ECE's responsibility to adults who lack the requisite content knowledge, instructional skills, and judgment needed to intentionally promote children's learning and development? To whom is ECE ultimately accountable?

These provocative questions are almost guaranteed to incite fierce reactions. Given the high stakes involved, choices will be emotionally difficult, even though, as Linsky and Heifetz (2007) point out, "adaptation and the process of doing adaptive work is as much about conservation and preservation as it is about loss" (p. x).

Organizing ECE as a professional field of practice involves more than adaptation, though. It also involves commitment to a different future. As Iyengar (2010) highlights in *The Art of Choosing,* "We are sculptors, finding ourselves in the evolution of choosing, not merely in the results of choice. When we change our thinking to embrace a more fluid process, choice will become no longer a force of destruction, an effort to break down what we don't want to be, but an ongoing, liberating act of creation" (p. 110).

## CAN WE? WILL WE?

Moving ahead demands leadership: mobilizing adaptive, systemic, and transformative work; implementing practices associated with effective leadership; managing the discomfort of uncertainty; and tirelessly pushing forward.

In their Foreword to *Ready or Not,* Linsky and Heifetz (2007) identified difficulties inherent to successfully engaging with the adaptive side of this work: It raises questions no one wants asked; it generates resistance, both active and passive by those with a stake in the status quo; and it makes many uncomfortable by holding them accountable for their role in the crisis at hand as well as for the solution.

I don't doubt that our field has the ability to tackle tough challenges. The lingering question is: Will we? As Linsky and Heifetz (2007) reflected, "Our guess is that the most powerful form of resistance will be to try to ignore the challenge because those in the early care and education system have accommodated to the status quo, made it work for them" (p. x).

As the Appendix reveals, this would not be an atypical response for ECE. The field has been characterized almost since its inception by pleas to address ambiguity regarding purpose, responsibility, and identity. Yet, responses have been too sporadic to engender the sustained dialogue needed for concerted action (Goffin, 2001).

Overcoming the field's historic inertia will not be easy. Acknowledging this reality, I find useful Fullan's (1998) elevation of the distinction between optimism and hope. Drawing on previous work that defined *hope* as "unwarranted optimism" (p. 8), Fullan quotes Vaclav Havel, the poet and former president of the Czech Republic:

> Hope is definitely not the same as optimism. It is not the conviction that something will turn out well, but the certainty that something makes sense, regardless of how it turns out. It is hope, above all, that gives us strength . . . to continually try new things, even in conditions that seem hopeless (p. 8).

Despite the complexity and difficulty of what lies ahead, consider me hopeful. ECE is resilient. It is a field of committed, caring, and smart individuals with a lengthy list of accomplishments achieved under challenging circumstances.

*ECE for a New Era* argues for forming ECE as a professional field of practice and engaging together in new ways to forge a different future for the field. It is different in its perspective because it looks to ECE to transform itself as a field of practice. It stresses the importance of the field's *collective* competence and highlights the necessity for choices if children are to have consistently effective early learning experiences.

Ultimately, *ECE for a New Era* is about our assuming responsibility and exercising leadership. As expressed by Kahane (2012), "It asks two fundamental and complementary questions that underlie all strategic planning: What is happening in the world that could have an impact on us? And what impact do we want to have on the world" (p. 68).

I am mindful of the discomfort and risk that come with raising the issues being put forth and the ease with which my words can be construed as judgmental, insensitive to others' hard work, and unappreciative of progress that has been made under difficult circumstances. To think otherwise would deny the dynamics involved when asking people to adapt to a new or challenging environment while envisioning a different future. Yet this is a defining moment for ECE as a field of practice:

- Too many children are losing ground and too many others are not accessing their potential.
- Notable gains exist in ECE's scientific knowledge base, but as a field of practice, they're neither widely understood nor applied.
- Increased expectations exist for ECE's contribution to children's successful Kindergarten entry, but the field lacks the ability to fulfill them.
- The field's increasingly complex systems of delivery, uneven funding, and variable standards require a more coherent approach for achieving consistent results across settings.
- Impatient with the field's relative passivity, others are stepping into the leadership void.

Will we embrace the opportunity to reset the field's trajectory?

## CHAPTER 2

# The Next Frontier: ECE as an Organized Field of Practice

*Ready or Not* argued that ECE should no longer delay responding to field-defining questions revolving around purpose and responsibility. Yet despite initial widespread interest, its call to action did little to propel active engagement with these still unresolved issues. This inaction is discouraging because it leaves unaddressed the field's contribution to a disturbing reality: A significant number of our nation's young children attend ECE programs that fail to promote their early learning and development (Barnett, 2011; Early et al., 2005; Shonkoff, 2011). According to a citation by Barnett (2011), between 35% and 45% of first time Kindergartners are ill prepared to succeed in school.

## ECE ON THE DEFENSIVE

Nonetheless, in the context of growing appreciation for its evidence-based potential to reduce educational gaps and promote success in later schooling, ECE has become the beneficiary of growing public support and financing. Early childhood advocates, often powered by philanthropic strategy and support, propelled this new status through public awareness campaigns, marketing efforts, targeted state and federal advocacy, and relentless relationship-building with "unlikely messengers" such as business leaders, police officials, and economists (Bruner, 2004; Pew Center on the States, 2011). As a result, ECE has grown dramatically in its visibility, exposing it to increasing public scrutiny regarding discrepancies between its overall results and those achieved by signature programs such as HighScope, the Abecedarian Project, and Chicago's Child Parent Centers.

As the public's appreciation for ECE expanded in response to growing awareness of early brain development and persuasive educational and financial results obtained from effective ECE programs, the field's disunity paved the way for caring and impatient philanthropists, business leaders, and federal and state policymakers to take the lead in finding ways to address the need for high-quality ECE programs. In the process, the field's contribution of specialized knowledge and practitioner expertise to program and systems development is being sidelined. ECE increasingly is the recipient of others' decisions, leaving it reactive to others' change agenda.

Rose's (2010) history of the Pre-Kindergarten movement offers a timely example in this regard. When describing the Pew Charitable Trusts' decision-making process for launching its 10-year initiative to make Pre-Kindergarten the start of public education, she concluded, "The way early education had developed—with limited public investment and infrastructure and relatively weak professional or stakeholder organizations—made it a good candidate for philanthropic involvement" (p. 138).

External intervention has entered the realm of practice, too. Reminiscent of the wave of researcher-conceived curriculum models developed in the 1970s and 1980s (Goffin & Wilson, 2001; White & Buka, 1987), present day researchers are tackling the challenge of unreliable teacher performance. Discouraged by uneven results from Pre-Kindergarten programs, frustrated by ineffective teacher preparation programs, and unmoved by arguments that 4-year degrees, at least as presently structured, will resolve the issue (Pianta, 2011, 2012), researchers committed to improving children's learning outcomes are devising programs to alter teacher behavior (e.g., Landry et al., 2006; Pianta, 2011; in a related vein see Mead & Carey, 2011). While their work has shifted attention from global constructs of program quality to teacher competence, their drive to improve practice through targeted training risks framing ECE as a technical occupation—even if not the intent.

# THE MISSING SYSTEM:
## ECE AS AN ORGANIZED FIELD OF PRACTICE

Exponential growth in ECE programs during the latter half of the 20th century, in conjunction with the call by governors to make school readiness the nation's first education goal (National Governor's Association, 1990), escalated interest in consistent quality across programs, equitable access, and results. In turn, this growth catalyzed thinking beyond discrete programs, leading to consideration of systematic approaches to providing ECE.

Thus, in the 1990s attention turned to systems building—to bringing coherence, coordination, and accountability to ECE's array of programs. These efforts were intensified in mid-2011 by the federal government's Race to the Top—Early Learning Challenge, a $500 million state-level competitive grant initiative designed to improve early learning and development programs for low income and disadvantaged children via creation and implementation of high quality integrated early learning and development systems (U.S. Department of Education & U.S. Department of Health and Human Services, 2011).

This 4-year, state-level systems building initiative (now extended to additional states) relies on states and the federal government to promote fieldwide systems change. If the grant's outcomes are to be achieved, however, attention also must be given to unifying ECE as a field of practice capable of providing consistent, competent practice across early learning and development programs, regardless of auspice or funding stream.

## QRIS as a Field Unifying Strategy

Some would argue that unifying ECE as a field of practice lies behind the obligation of winning states to expand their Quality Rating and Improvement Systems (QRISs) and broaden participation to include all ECE programs. Based on state-determined policies (Mitchell, 2012), a QRIS is a standards-based, systematic approach for assessing, improving, and communicating the level of quality in ECE programs. RAND researchers Zellman and Karoly (2012) identified three factors to explain the growth of QRIS, two of which closely match fieldwide issues already identified:

1. Continuing gaps in quality in existing ECE programs;
2. The inability of ECE's present system to promote uniformly high quality; and
3. Features of the ECE market that limit consumption of high quality services.

QRIS has evolved since its inception in the 1990s. It has progressed from a subsidy-based, quality improvement incentive for child care programs to a coordinating structure for diverse child care settings to, most recently, a structure imbued with the potential to unify ECE's diverse array of programs and program supports around common standards and tiered performance levels.

It has to be remembered, though, that participation in QRIS is typically voluntary. In addition to challenges associated with motivating broad involvement, participating programs may choose to perform indefinitely at levels below what are known to promote children's development and preparation for Kindergarten. Further, since premised on market-driven principles, parents may choose to rely on programs rated as providing low quality—albeit for reasons not always reflecting their preferences. Additionally, QRISs rely on financing from state governments, which typically target public funds to vulnerable and low-income children—potentially omitting a broad group of children.

Enthusiasm for QRIS revolves around its potential to promote program improvements and unify ECE programs around a common set of standards—at least within individual states. Researchers are delving into whether and how QRIS effects changes in children's school readiness; to date, though, "little research and evaluation has focused on whether and to what extent QRIS serve this centralizing function in early childhood systems" (Tout, 2013, p. 74).

QRIS is relatively young and evolving. Still, even if one detours around the absence of research documenting QRIS as a preferential strategy for elevating program quality statewide and skims over complexities associated with implementation and monitoring, the span of QRIS's scope and authority calls into question whether it can fulfill the aspiration of unifying ECE as a field of practice. Given its design, the ability of QRIS to mend the fragmentation of purpose and responsibility that undermines ECE's collective competence and promote systemization as a field of practice seems questionable.

## Early Learning Standards as a Field Unifying Strategy

Reflecting growing awareness that ECE's fragmented practice needs to be addressed, Kagan (2012) has proposed that early learning standards perform this unifying function. Defined as policy statements of what children should know and be able to do, she suggests that early learning standards can provide the basis for improving pedagogy, curriculum, and teacher preparation curricula. A plus is that learning standards don't dictate curricula and methods but rather permit proof of effectiveness to reside in what children learn (Bowman, 2007). Citing their catalytic effect in other countries, Kagan (2012) characterized early learning standards as an elixir for early childhood systems reform.

Kagan's field-unifying proposal recognizes the importance of addressing inconsistencies in ECE as a field of practice, a form of fieldwide fragmentation receiving less attention than incoherence derived from uncoordinated public policies and service delivery systems. She argues that early learning standards can be used to form a coherent early childhood pedagogical subsystem that, in turn, can underpin an integrated approach to ECE. Echoing a theme found in Goffin (2012) and this book, she contends, "no matter how well governed, funded, credentialed, and assessed the early childhood system and its participants are, advancements will remain haphazard and unrealized unless there is some intellectual core holding the field together" (Kagan, 2012, p. 67).

ECE as a professional field of practice extends beyond an organizing framework, however, and also functions as more than a contributing subsystem. As a field-unifying strategy, professions create a *system* for preparation and practice that is fieldwide, coheres subsystems, and is field-led. Professions are organized not only around an intellectual core, but also around ethical obligations, which together shape a field's shared identity.

Additionally, while relying on authorization that comes from supportive public policies, professions shift leadership and accountability responsibilities to those directly engaged with supporting children's learning and development. Professions enter into a social contract that obligates them as fields of practice to assume responsibility for their collective performance and to serve as an "independent moral voice in evaluating social policies" (Freidson, 2001, p. 197).

## Public Policy: Determinant or Lever

State-based efforts to build ECE professional development systems, guided by the National Association for the Education of Young Children's (NAEYC) policy blueprint (LeMoine, 2008), provide another example of the field's propensity to rely on public policy to catalyze change *within* ECE. State policies perform a crucial legitimizing and authorizing—and often financing—role for professions. By looking to public policy in the area of professional development, however, ECE jeopardizes a profession's core responsibility to prepare its practitioners, a duty uniformly recognized as a profession's obligation (Dower, O'Neil, & Hough, 2001;

Freidson, 2001; Sullivan, 2005a, 2005b). By relying on state and federal policymakers to provoke and approve fieldwide change related to the practice of ECE, the field relinquishes a profession's core responsibility, regardless of how often ECE leaders are convened for input.

Legislative and administrative policies obviously are powerful and strategic agents for change. Yet policy formation occurs within a complex decision-making process driven by interests and constraints not always aligned with, or even supportive of, the field's research base or aspirations (Bellm & Whitebook, 2006; Morgan, 2001; Rose, 2010; Zigler, Marsland, & Lord, 2009). Reliance on policy to advance ECE means the trigger for fieldwide change comes more and more from advocates and government, not, as is the case of other professions, from a field's articulation of the policy supports necessary to ensure its competence and accessibility are aligned with public needs (Goffin, 2009).

Being lifted for consideration is the dominance and consequence of public policy increasingly defining and managing ECE: Should public policy steer ECE's development as a field of practice or should it play an enabling, partnership role? Should ECE become a regulated civil service occupation or should it assume responsibility, with its accompanying obligations, for choosing its organizing structure and standards for practice?

## Calling the Question

Despite massive efforts and investments directed at building statewide ECE systems since the 1990s, consequential change has been elusive, in part because as a field we've not attended to the field of practice for which, and around which, ECE's delivery and policy systems should be developed and coordinated (Goffin, 2012). Though rarely acknowledged explicitly, ECE's systems building work and efforts to better nurture and educate children have been weakened not only by disjointed policies and delivery systems but also by ECE's presence as a disorganized field of practice—or said differently, by ECE's absence as an organized field of practice.

While it can be argued that the multiplicity of co-existing visions for ECE are natural artifacts of the field's multiple histories, it can as easily be claimed that this variety reveals the absence of a clearly delineated field of practice organized around shared purpose and articulated responsibilities (Goffin, 2012). Participants in systems building activities in states and communities routinely are subjected to the confusion, frustration, and limited results that come from seemingly unending and circular debates. What typically gets described as the complexity of systems building should as often be recognized as the turmoil generated by the field's identity issues and lack of clarity about purpose and responsibility.

This inconsistency contributes to the mixed design of system building efforts and to uneven performance expectations for practitioners. Absent an organized field of practice, state and community systems building efforts are hampered in attempts to construct systems and policies that serve a clearly articulated purpose.

Of the three field-unifying strategies—QRIS, early learning standards, and professionalism—systematizing ECE as a profession is the only one focused on mending a fragmented field of practice by unifying its practitioners around consistency of purpose, competent practice, and shared responsibility. As Rhodes and Huston (2012) argued, focusing solely on professional development strategies to produce a competent workforce is insufficient. Consistently high quality ECE relies on the collective competence of its practitioners (IOM & NRC, 2012; Rhodes & Huston, 2012; Phillips & Lowenstein, 2011; Pianta, 2012).

## The Significance of Common Purpose

Needed for the basic work of connecting the field's disparate parts into a coherent profession is finding common purpose (Dower, O'Neil, & Hough, 2001; Goffin & Washington, 2007; Kurtzman, 2010; Ready & Truelove, 2011; Senge, 1990). On the one hand, this means "one needs to know what the profession aims to do" (Dower, O'Neil, & Hough, 2001, p. 5), and on the other, it means "the capacity to hold a shared picture of the future we seek to create" (Senge, 1990, p. 9).

A prominent systems thinker, Senge (1990) stressed that a system's organizing structure is crucial but by itself insufficient. "By itself, it lacks a sense of purpose. It deals with the *how*, not the *why*" (p. 354, emphasis in original). Building an effective ECE system, therefore, requires grounding in a clear understanding of what is being nurtured, delivered, monitored, and sustained. Thus in an inversion of current thinking, coordinated systems of delivery and policy depend on ECE as an organized field of practice.

ECE's future awaits our choices. ECE can mobilize itself to address internal issues and take responsibility for forming its future—and thereby contribute more effectively to children's futures—or it can sidestep organizing as a professional field of practice and firmly establish ECE as a field largely shaped by others.

## PARTING WAYS WITH ECE'S HABITS OF MIND

Spodek, Saracho, and Peters (1988) asserted that failure of the field's various strands "to come together under one conceptualization of early childhood education is central to understanding the debate surrounding issues of professionalism" (p. 3). But why is this so? Why has ECE yet to come together around a shared conceptualization of purpose and responsibility to children and families?

In an attempt to answer these questions, four "habits of mind" or mental models restraining the field's advancement are proposed. A systems-thinking term, "mental models are deeply ingrained assumptions, generalizations, or even pictures or images that influence how we understand the world and how we take action" (Senge, 1990, p. 8).

Mental models are deeply entrenched; so typically we are not consciously aware of them or their effects on our behavior. Consequently, "The discipline of working with mental models starts with turning the mirror inward; learning to unearth our internal pictures of the world, to bring them to the surface and hold them rigorously to scrutiny" (Senge, 1990, p. 9).

### Habits of Mind: Mindsets that Constrain Us

The proposed habits of mind that follow can be attributed to a complex interplay of the field's origins and sociocultural and political contexts:

1. Timidity as a field of practice;
2. Resistance to distinctive scopes of practice;
3. An evangelical orientation; and
4. Dependency on others to advance the field's merit.

Although sometimes characterized by contradictory tendencies, as an ensemble these habits of mind illuminate ECE's seeming unresponsiveness to calls for coming together around shared purpose and obligations to children and families.

***Timidity as a field of practice.*** Throughout its history, ECE has circumvented organizing as a coherent field of practice—in contrast to fields such as nursing and social work, both female dominated, that emerged at about the same time (Goffin, 2009). Early educators didn't initially seek professional status (Bredekamp & Goffin, 2012). From its onset in the 1920s, however, the nursery school movement—which still largely supplies ECE's philosophical underpinnings and guides its pedagogical approach—identified its work as professional (Hewes et al., 2001; Lazerson, 1972). Yet this self-designation has not resulted in a professional structure despite repeated calls for action (see the Appendix), leading Schoenlkopf to exclaim in opening remarks to NANE's (National Association for Nursery Education, forerunner to the National Association for the Education of Young Children [NAEYC]) biannual conference in 1957, "I consider my role to be that of a "provocative protagonist" and "catalytic agent." It is earnestly hoped that in playing such a role, the profession of preschool educators will be stimulated to *come of age!"* (p. 9, emphasis in original).

Following transfer in 1981 of the Child Development Associate (CDA) program from the independent Child Development Associate Consortium to Bank Street College, NAEYC Board President Barbara Bowman (1981) noted that the transfer broke the relationship between CDA and the professional organizations that formed it. This led members to question NAEYC's role "in relation to all credentials, licenses, state requirements, certificates, and other awards designated to attest to professional competency" (p. 56).

In response, the NAEYC Governing Board established "an Early Childhood Credentialing Commission with the charge to make recommendations regarding the feasibility of a credentialing system for all levels of professional practice . . . and ways to organize and implement such a system" (p. 57). What resulted, however, was a voluntary recognition system for ECE programs. Preservice guidelines for baccalaureate degree programs were under development, and the Commission recommended an early childhood program accreditation system as a complementary structure.[1]

In 1989, NAEYC identified "tough" issues in need of attention (Smith, 1989, p. 32). A strategic planning process was announced that was to include in-depth exploration of the question, "How do we define our profession?" (p. 36)—an exploration that never materialized. Then, in 1991, as child care attendance escalated and concern grew over uneven program quality, the Carnegie Corporation of New York awarded NAEYC a grant to develop consensus around professional development with the intent of advancing the field's collective competence and professionalism (National Institute for Early Childhood Professional Development, 1993). In 1995, when the multi-year funding ended, the initiative faded—although state-level work catalyzed by this effort continues with support from NAEYC.

This brief review–tied so much to NAEYC because of its historical relationship with the nursery school movement and its tenets of professionalism–indicates that sustained attention has not been given to formalizing ECE as an organized field of practice. Reticence to step forward as a field of practice, however, is undercutting the ability to form a shared identity, determine mutual responsibilities, and mobilize collective change to address the field's uneven performance.

**Resistance to distinctive scopes of practice.** Drawing from the nursing profession, a scope of practice statement "describes the *who, what, where, when, why, and how*" of practice. Each of these questions," according to the American Nurses Association, "must be sufficiently answered to provide a complete picture of the practice and its boundaries and membership" (American Nurses Association, 2004, p. 1, emphasis in original).

ECE's long-standing support for the "whole child," when extending beyond the field's signature whole child curricular and pedagogical beliefs, blurs boundaries between ECE's distinctive contribution to children resulting from its specialized knowledge base and its holistic commitment to children's development. As a result, any course of study within one of several disciplines focused on children is typically accepted for teacher preparation (Maxwell, Lim, & Early, 2006), symbolized by the "early childhood-related" label widely applied when identifying training and preparation requirements (Whitebook et al., 2012).

This lack of clarity encourages uncertainty regarding the field's reason for being, confusion about its distinctive responsibility to children, and reluctance to establish boundaries. As expressed by Stendler (1952) when articulating the responsibilities of preschool teachers, "The classroom teacher should recognize that she is not solely responsible for all aspects of child growth and development" (p. 14)–and the same might be said for ECE as a field of practice. As more recently noted by Shonkoff (2010) in conjunction with efforts to craft a social strategy to gain public support for early childhood development, ECE is not the same as early childhood development in terms of focus or intentionality.

**An evangelical orientation.** On the one hand, ECE's impulse to "save" children in need (Cravens, 1985; Finkelstein, 1988; Lazerson, 1972)–often carried over to the adults who care for them–and on the other, eagerness to reform public education and society (Antler, 1987; Biber, 1984; White & Buka, 1987), foster what Finkelstein (1988) called the field's "moral evangelicism" (p. 13). Deeply embedded dispositions, the early intervention programs of the 1960s further entrenched this mindset and, according to Takanishi (1977) undergirded Head Start's initial formation as a social action program organized around child-saving.

Humanitarian concern for children is, of course, a fundamental value, and improving public education is also imperative. Yet in the context of "moral evangelicism" the field's missionary zeal (Tobin, 1992) can imbue us with a sense of self-righteousness, inhibiting internal change while also fostering an expectation that it's primarily the obligation of others to change.

***Dependency on others to advance the field's merit.*** Since the 1930s, but most especially since the mid-60s and the onset of Head Start, ECE has grown in tandem with the nation's early childhood policy agenda. Typically serving as a surrogate for societal reform (Cravens, 1993; Grubb & Lazerson, 1982, 1988; Lazerson, 1971; White & Buka, 1987), this relationship has fostered reliance on policy to effect fieldwide change. This mindset was strengthened when public will building emerged as a strategy for influencing family and child policy options (see The Children's Partnership, 1996; Coalition for America's Children, 1999; Mitchell & Shore, 1999). More recently, this strategy is being used to cultivate business leaders and others as early childhood champions (The Pew Center on the States, 2011).

As a result, the field's development and what is seen as worthy in terms of forming ECE as a field of practice is being driven by the unpredictable processes of policy making and decision making among federal and state government agencies. Limiting internal change to what the general public and policymakers will support promotes dependence on others. It also provides the basis for affirming what is worthwhile about the field's work.

Reliance on public policy for effecting fieldwide change has politicized ECE and prioritized programs and practices aligned with political interests and the boundaries of public policy (Fuller, 2007; Fuller & Holloway, 1996; Garwood et al., 1989; Morgan, 2001; Rose, 2010). Framing ECE primarily in terms of policy has positioned advocates as the face and voice of the field, restricting development as a field of practice.

Posing this last habit of mind, in particular, risks my being interpreted as judgmental, critical of early childhood advocates, and naïve about the crucial role of politics and policy. This interpretation would miss the mark, though. The field does not want to disrupt its increasingly effective advocacy. Nonetheless, a difference in intent has to be articulated: Advocacy should be for the purpose of changing policy conditions that restrain ECE's development, effectiveness, and access to its services. Yet in the absence of ECE as an organized field of practice, advocates are defining the field's purpose and responsibility. ECE's absence as an organized field of practice is reducing its options to grow as a specialized domain of practice.

## The Importance of Boundaries

These habits of mind help explain the field's growing status as reactor versus actor in responding to the question of "What defines and bounds ECE as a field of practice?" Yet answering this question is central to articulating the field's commitment to children and families. "Holism, in the sense of including everything, is an impossibility. Every endeavor has to set boundaries—make choices between which relationships to include and which to exclude, which perspectives to honor and which to marginalize. Setting boundaries is not optional" (Williams, 2011, p. 4).

Sidestepping the question of ECE's boundaries dilutes development as an articulated field of practice with clarity regarding collective obligations to children's early learning and development. "The formation of boundaries . . . allows members to focus on a common body of formal knowledge and skill, or discipline. Without boundaries, nothing that could be appropriately called even an occupation, let alone a formal discipline, could exist" (Freidson, 2001, p. 202).

## MOVING FORWARD AS A FIELD OF PRACTICE

Since its inception during the mid-1800s to early 1900s, the rise and fall of public interest; splintered programs, policies, and funding; increases in demand; and more recently, the field's increased politicization have been superimposed on a field chronically underdeveloped as a domain of practice.

*ECE for a New Era* argues that ECE should step forward to assume greater responsibility for the field's destiny. Yes, the need for durable financing is crucial, but even resolving this challenge is hampered by the field's fragmented state.

ECE can move forward as a field of practice by:

- Forming the field as a coherent, competent, and accountable profession;
- Building fieldwide leadership to ensure a leadership infrastructure exists to address issues of fieldwide import; and
- Embedding leadership development into the field's culture and practice so ECE has capacity to grow and thrive.

## The Next Frontier

White and Buka (1987) described the field's development prior to Head Start as a research and development sequence with different versions of ECE emerging from practical needs, private and governmental projects, and insights from philosophy, educational ideologies, and utopian programs.

> The early educators visited and borrowed; they wrote down their ideas and methods; they lectured and proselytized; they had disciples; they started teacher training programs. Their scattered ventures were fused into a tradition—a community of people linked across space and time whose common cause was early education. (p. 43)

Borrowing from White and Buka's description, ECE's first developmental phase can be categorized as one of "Establishing Traditions." As Lazerson noted (1972), "Although variations existed in practice, a pedagogical orthodoxy was being enunciated" (p. 48), an orthodoxy later codified in NAEYC's position statements on developmentally appropriate practice (Bredekamp, 1986; Copple & Bredekamp, 2009).

The field's second developmental phase is easily associated with the onset of Head Start in 1964, which repeatedly is recognized as a pivotal event in ECE's development (Barnett, 1993; Clarke-Stewart, 1988; White & Buka, 1987). This phase, which can be characterized as one of "Expanded Policies and Programs," was a time of great excitement about the potential for social change, heightened involvement by the federal government, growth in programs, and development of diverse curriculum models and research on their efficacy (Goffin & Wilson, 2001).

ECE's third and still evolving phase of development—"Systems Building and Self-Realization"—can be tagged to the 1990s when the field's growth fostered a shift from program expansion to system building. In question, though, is whether ECE will use this developmental phase to fuel self-realization as a competent field of practice.

Self-realization as a professional field of practice is ECE's next frontier. Like any frontier, it is uncharted territory. Yet, entering into this new territory offers ECE leadership opportunities with significant consequence for children and society.

Forming ECE as a profession can propel the field toward fulfilling its potential–as well as children's. This organizational work is essential to unifying as a field of practice, fostering competence regardless of program or auspice, and moderating inconsistencies caused by diverse delivery systems, public policies, and state-by-state variations.

Realizing this opportunity will require ECE to articulate boundaries. Inevitably, this step will lead to discussions about the personal mastery expected of those within the field's boundaries in terms of (1) knowledge, skills, and dispositions for effective practice and (2) obligations associated with being an early childhood educator–not because it is demanded by discrete public policies serving targeted populations of children, but because those who choose to become early educators commit to values and performance expectations that define ECE as a field of practice accountable to every child.

## Claiming the Field's Voice

Issacs (1999), a master of dialogue, defined *voice* as expressing what needs to be said–of revealing what is true for you regardless of other influences that might be brought to bear. Voicing, as he calls it, can be individual or represent a group of people.

Indicative of its unstructured state, throughout the field's evolution it has lacked a sustained, knowledgeable, and organized fieldwide voice guiding practitioners to increasingly competent and responsible levels of practice and steering policy as a partner in achieving its ambitions for the nation's children.

Weber (1969) made note of this gap when she bemoaned the curricular changes being foisted upon Kindergarten in the 1960s: "No single arena for debating issues and determining new directions exists in the sixties as it did at the turn of the century. . . . The fragmentation of leadership plus the diversity of points of view complicate the process of reconstructing the kindergarten program" (pp. 209–210).

ECE has been blessed with a multitude of individual voices that express important and insightful views on the field's aspirations and concerns, and who individually have made–and are making–significant contributions to ECE (see, for example, NAEYC, 2001; Neugebauer,

1995; Snyder, 1972–not to mention the leadership that elevated ECE to its present public and policy status). Yet the field has lacked one strong voice,[2] marginalizing sustained advancements tied to an expanding knowledge base and undermining a collective response to the uneven performance characterizing ECE.

To be clear: The call for organizing and unifying ECE as a field of practice does not mean that ECE's future can or should be solely the field's responsibility or that the dynamic changes occurring around us can or should be ignored. As Heifetz (1994) cautioned, "To produce adaptive change, a vision must track the contours of reality; it has to have accuracy, and not simply imagination and appeal" (p. 24).

Yet without the unified, countervailing voice of those whose work revolves around a commitment to the quality and effectiveness of children's early learning experiences, ECE is being redefined in ways unsupported by its science and legacy of effective practices. Widespread concern exists for misuse of child assessments, the denigration and disappearance of play, the impact of national core standards, and disregard for developmentally appropriate instructional practices. As expressed by a discouraged colleague, "ECE is losing its soul."

This doesn't have to be ECE's fate. Coalescing around our collective possibility and transforming ECE as a professional field of practice can prompt a different future.

## CHAPTER 3

# Forming ECE as a Profession

ECE's fragmentation as a field of practice undermines its capacity to effectively educate and care for children. Its splintered form promotes variability in individual proficiency and weakens the quality and effectiveness of children's early learning experiences. Professions are purposely structured to address this problematic situation.

Upon confronting the field's reluctance to professionalize in the early 1990s, Bredekamp (1992a) reminded us that "When individuals who are responsible for the care and education of children remain ignorant of the knowledge base, children pay the price. Although we [referring to the NAEYC National Institute for Early Childhood Professional Development] are committed to maintaining access, we must be more committed to maintaining quality for children. We must continue to learn with and from children, but we must stop learning *on* children" (pp. 53–54, emphasis in original).

## THE NEXT FRONTIER AWAITS

In an edited volume on professionalism published in 1988, Haberman asserted, "In no case . . . is the dislocation between the field–as practiced–and the expertise–as professed–as great as it is in early childhood education" (p. 91). This dislocation, unfortunately, remains intact (Barnett, 2011; Pianta, Barnett, Burchinal, & Thornburg, 2009), contributing to poor results for children and reduced respect for ECE's work.

Reversing this reality is long overdue. Prior to ECE's exponential growth and the public's interest in educational outcomes and return on investment, the field's disconnected state was easily ignored. Indicative that this no longer is the case, efforts are underway in almost every state to build professional development systems, construct career lattices, implement early learning standards, and establish QRISs–each with the intent of improving program quality and consequences for children.

These change strategies, however, do not address issues of purpose and boundaries, remedy uneven preparation, or articulate fieldwide obligations to children and families. Professions do. Professions address these fundamental issues by introducing interlocking systemic features that unify disorganized fields around shared purpose, competent practice, and ethical commitments.

The time has come to form ECE as a *system of preparation and practice*, moving beyond voluntary improvement strategies and coordination of training and preparation programs irrespective of content and effectiveness.

## Platforms for Moving Forward

Change strategies underway to increase ECE's competence offer platforms for boosting the field into its next frontier. Those serving as architects and change agents have valuable knowledge and skills to contribute. Emerging structures and lessons learned from facilitating college completion and from designing and implementing professional development systems, career lattices, and QRISs offer stepping-stones for moving ECE forward as a profession.

These endeavors can be joined with other change strategies en route to professionalism, such as accreditation for ECE programs and for two- and four-year preparation programs. Further, quality improvement activities have aroused receptivity to classroom and program enhancements, directed attention to child outcomes, and introduced system thinking to the field. These accomplishments can be used to advance ECE's capabilities.

## Progressing Together

As a field in search of increased coherence, consistency, and impact, ECE can be proud of its progress. By stretching beyond present thinking and organizing as a profession, the field has even stronger potential for promoting effective practice across individuals and settings, raising the status of its work, and creating a sustainable infrastructure.

Doing so, however, requires moving beyond appropriating professional terminology and summoning the will to become a profession in form and practice. As Goodlad noted (1990), "A vocation is not a profession just because those in it choose to call it one. It must be recognized as such" (p.

29). Neglecting this distinction hampers us from seizing a powerful strategy for unifying ECE and improving its collective competence.

This chapter looks at motivations that have mobilized other fields of practice to professionalize and identifies central features of professions, highlighting structural elements ECE will need to address while also acknowledging tensions they will evoke. Building on this foundation, Chapter 4 delves deeper into historical antecedents, further illuminating the pathway that brought ECE to its present crossroad. Then it offers a framework for conceptualizing ECE as an organized field of practice, attending to individual competence, solidarity[1] of purpose, and professional identity—what Sullivan (2010) called the *raison d'etre* of a profession.

Recall from Chapter 1, though, that *ECE for a New Era* does not detail the particulars of ECE as a profession, such as requisite knowledge and skills. The myriad choices required to transform to a profession necessitates shared work. The aspirations being expressed cannot possibly be achieved without the unity that "binds us together in a mutual and continuing pursuit of a higher purpose" (Burns, 2010/1978, p. 20).

## Other Occupational Forms

Two other forms or types of occupations can be identified in addition to professions (Freidson, 2001): those organized and driven by the free market and those organized and managed by government and managerial/corporate organizations. While not the intent to delve into sociological distinctions among occupational forms, their distinctions can be instructive for understanding ECE's present occupational status.

Differences among occupational types revolve around five elements: an occupation's social identity; its division of labor (how work is organized around different tasks); reliance on different types of knowledge and skill; entry expectations; and with whom "control" over one's work resides—consumers, managers/supervisors, or the occupation. Of the three occupation types, only professions are privileged with articulating their body of knowledge and granted authority over its use in practice. As *systems* with an institutional infrastructure and fieldwide leadership for guiding practice and ensuring continuing integrity, professions represent a distinct way of organizing work (Freidson, 2001).

Given its range of sponsors and funding, ECE might best be characterized as a mixture of (1) free market/competition, where consumers largely drive the work that people do and cost is driven by competitive forces (e.g., child care) and (2) managerially-driven work, encompassing all formal organizations, including government agencies, where those in managerial roles oversee the work, set goals, and establish evaluative criteria, thereby determining the boundaries within which expertise may be expressed (e.g., Head Start).

These occupational forms are best understood as prototypes for distinguishing among occupations because they don't exist in pure form. QRISs provide an example that blends free market values with government oversight. The expanding presence of ECE in managerial organizations (e.g., United Ways, Chambers of Commerce) provides an example of where employers establish parameters for how the field's knowledge base can be applied by employees. Absent is an example of ECE as a full-fledged profession given responsibility for developing its knowledge base and exercising authority over its use in practice.

## WHY OCCUPATIONS ORGANIZE AS PROFESSIONS

Examination of a wide range of other fields reveals relative consistency in motivations for organizing as a profession. To varying degrees, each seeks the coherence, sense of purpose, autonomy, improved performance, and social recognition that organizing as a profession offers.

In documenting professionalization of psychology, Camfield (1973) emphasized desire for autonomy and recognition as an independent branch of a larger discipline. Like psychology, the field of health law seeks recognition as a distinctive branch within a larger discipline, one with internal coherence, improved effectiveness, and increased clarity about its approach to law and relationship to other subspecialties (Elhauge, 2006).

Nursing, which like ECE confronts the challenge of working across a wide range of settings and auspices, organized as a profession in the late 1800s to promote professional and educational advancement of nurses and present a united front on issues affecting nursing and the welfare of nurses (Flanagan, 1976). In the present, dramatic changes in technology, the economy, and health care delivery are driving nursing to confront contentious issues of nurse preparation and scopes of practice associated with differing levels of preparation (Goffin, 2009), making it a particularly relevant informant to ECE.

Following 50 years of public policies that elevated its social importance, forestry was driven by a sense of social responsibility as well as desire for autonomy, increased competence, and consistent performance.

"As professional foresters, we cannot be willing victims of economic cir-cumstances or simply the hired hands of our employers. We have a social responsibility the discharge of which should be our pride" (Zivnuska, 1963, pp. 339–340).

Identifying themselves as the world's newest profession, financial planners view the knowledge and skills embedded in their services as essential to individual financial well-being (Brandon & Welch, 2009). To fulfill this aspiration, financial planners labored for over 40 years to transcend their industrial roots and distinguish themselves from other financial services by exercising a fiduciary standard of care and by de-veloping ways for identifying individuals with the requisite knowledge, skills, and fiduciary accountability to offer financial planning guidance (Goffin, 2009).

More recently, policing is considering professionalism as a vehicle for increased legitimacy, evidence based practice and innovation, account-ability to stakeholders, and national coherence (Stone & Travis, 2011). Social entrepreneurship is seeking to create coherence and credibility, advance knowledge and practice, and create a dynamic field of practice (Center for Advancement of Social Entrepreneurship, 2008).

Finally, the field of business is questioning its contribution to the inter-national financial crisis. Khurana and Nohria (2008), both Harvard Busi-ness School faculty, call for making management a true profession, one that recognizes fiduciary responsibilities to society and defines an implicit social contract among members of the profession toward a higher-order purpose. Prahalad (2010) frames the need for business to professionalize in terms of managers' responsibility as custodians of society's most powerful institutions, while Pfeffer (2011) stresses the importance of tying higher-order aspirations to a specialized body of knowledge that practitioners are obliged to use in their daily work.

Beyond revealing consistent rationales for organizing as a profes-sion, these examples highlight that ECE is not unique in having to grap-ple with issues of purpose, coherence, and performance accountability. Further, fields newly contemplating professionalism are not deterred by the fact that professions are evolving in their form. No longer, for ex-ample, do most professions have complete autonomy over their practice or financing—once prominent features of professions. Professionals now practice within corporate entities (e.g., corporate lawyers; physicians working for hospitals) and often rely on third party payment systems.

Nor have all professions fully retained their signature service mis-sion and orientation, leading proponents of professionalism to bemoan the impact of market forces on professions' moral underpinning and to lament their weakened ability to govern development and use of their specialized knowledge and skill (Gardner & Schulman, 2005; Freidson, 2001; Metzger, 1987; Sullivan, 2005a, 2005b). Assessing this state of affairs, Freidson (2001) lamented that professions were at risk of "preserving form without spirit" (p. 181).

Still, as a uniquely organized form of work, professions have retained their distinctive occupational obligation: preparing individuals with specialized knowledge and the capability and autonomy to bring judgment to bear in its application, guided by a strong sense of moral accountability (Freidson, 2001; Metzger, 1987; Sullivan, 2005a). After 10 years of studying the professions of law, engineering, clergy, nursing, and medicine, Sullivan (2005a) concluded, "The great promise of the professions has always been that they can ensure the quality of expert services for the common good. At the same time, the professions have also offered individuals the possibility of a form of self-actualization as workers, as citizens, and as persons—and the hope of a career in which one's livelihood is good for others as well as oneself" (p. 25).

## Concerns For What May Be Lost

In explaining professions as organized fields of practice, sociologist Freidson (2001) acknowledged, "virtues are always accompanied by unanticipated vices" (p. 2). Choices are not risk free, and the construct of professionalism is evolving in response to changing political, social, technological, and economic circumstances (Freidson, 2001; Dower, O'Neil, & Hough, 2001; Gardner & Schulman, 2005; Sullivan, 2005a, 2005b). Some of these shifts respond (or are responding) to concerns expressed by the ECE field, such as attributing expertise solely to professionals, emphasizing theory and research to the exclusion of practical wisdom, prompting disparity between professionals and "clients," disregarding context, and marking entry into a profession as an end point versus the start of one's learning journey (Morgan, 1994b[2]; Spodek, Saracho, & Peters, 1988; VanderVen, 1994).

Other expressed concerns can be addressed in the context of formulating a professional structure for ECE. It may be helpful at this point to recall that adaptive change—engaging in problem-solving work in the midst of adaptive pressures—displaces and rearranges "some old DNA" (Heifetz, Grashow, & Linsky, 2009, p. 16) but also holds onto those beliefs and loyalties essential to a field's core identity. Adaptive change isn't accomplished, though, without making choices and confronting the inevitable: the discomfort inherent to the process, including that what one person views as positive change can result in another person feeling incompetent or irrelevant.

Research suggests that concern for losses can be more powerful than anticipation of gains (Iyengar, 2010). Yet at stake is the field's integrity (Goffin & Washington, 2007). Once the present is no longer viewed as acceptable, though, adaptive and transformative possibilities will become more visible (Kahane, 2012).

## ECE's Concerns

Historically, six concerns have thwarted organizing ECE as a profession. These overlapping concerns are listed below, accompanied by embedded questions. They expose anxiety over losses tied to four values: (1) attending to the whole child; (2) access by adults wishing to be caregivers and teachers; (3) partnership relationships with families; and (4) commitment to serving children from poor families (Bredekamp, 1992a; Bredekamp & Willer, 1993; Freeman & Feeney, 2006; Morgan, 1994a, 1994b; Spodek, Saracho, & Peters, 1988; Urban, 2010; VanderVen, 1994).

1. *Separating "care" from "education"*: Will professionalizing ECE result in the loss of caring relationships as a foundational tenet? Will child care be separated from education and isolated from the rest of the field?
2. *Diminished focus on the whole child*: Will professionalizing ECE standardize practice and minimize responsiveness to individual and cultural differences? Will children's social and emotional development be marginalized? Will openness to collaborating with other child- and family-focused disciplines be undermined?
3. *Access*: Will professionalizing ECE result in programs being excluded or narrow the ages of children being served? Can a profession encompass the field's extensive variety? How will ECE personnel, programs, and families be affected?
4. *Admittance*: Will professionalizing ECE leave out some people? Who will be defined as a professional? Who will be "in" and who will be "out"? Will multiple entry points into the field still be available? Will fixed entry requirements preclude movement into other roles? How will the field's expanding number of roles be incorporated? Given racial, ethnic, linguistic, and economic

barriers, how will the field ensure that teachers reflect the diversity of children and families with whom they work?

5. *Field-based relationships:* Will professionalizing ECE foster a status system within programs and/or among the field's sectors? Will distinctions among professionals, non-, pre-, or paraprofessionals create a status system? Will different expectations for preparation create status differences among practitioners?

6. *Increased costs:* Recruiting and retaining qualified teaching staff requires higher compensation levels. Where will financial resources come from, and how will "solutions" impact parent access to good ECE programs?

## Stepping Forward

ECE is on the cusp of a pivotal leadership opportunity. As the questions listed above make evident, conflict will be inevitable. It is an inescapable consequence of transformational and adaptive change (Burns, 2010/1978; Heifetz, 1994; Heifetz, Grashow, & Linsky, 2009). It is also a crucible for moving forward. "Leadership," according to Burns (2010/1978), "acts as an inciting and triggering force in the conversion of conflicting demands, values, and goals into significant behavior" (p. 38).

Ultimately, the field's choice is whether to become an active force in shaping ECE's future or acquiesce to others to forge ECE as a field of practice. Choices about organizational structure need not mirror other professions, an oft-cited concern. A profession can be formed that encompasses a field's core values.

Still, while room exists for attending to ECE's values (Bredekamp, 1992a; Freeman & Feeney, 2006; Morgan, 1994b; Sykes, 1987; Vander-Ven, 1994), achieving shared purpose and coherence and maximizing the field's potential require retention of characteristics that distinguish a profession from other occupational forms. In particular, confronting thorny questions associated with admittance cannot be dodged. As Rhodes and Huston (2012) noted, "The low status afforded ECCE [referring to early care and education] work seems to reflect the belief that little separates ECCE caregivers from babysitters and parents who generally care for children without special training, particularly in settings that are not designed with an educational focus" (p. 12).

Acknowledgement of expert authority, marked by credentials or certification/licensure, is central to recognition as a profession (Dower,

O'Neil, & Hough, 2001; Freidson, 2001; Sullivan, 2005b). Professions are comprised of individuals with effective command over a defined body of knowledge and skill, requiring admission qualifications and affirmation of the right to practice. These professional functions underpin professional accountability to children, families, policymakers, and to each other.

Often maligned as monopolism, Freidson (2001) countered, "The monopoly of professionalism is not over real property, wealth, political power, or even knowledge, but rather over the *practice* of a defined body of intellectualized knowledge and skill, a discipline" (p. 198, emphasis in original). While unlikely to have a monopoly over its practice given its multi-disciplinary knowledge base, the field's ability to apply its developmental and pedagogical knowledge is nonetheless eroding as policymakers and others increasingly dictate ECE practices and expected outcomes.

Experience teaches us that issues of entry requirements, credentials, and certification/licensure will be contentious (Bredekamp, 2004; Neugebauer, 2011; Willer & Bredekamp, 1993; Zigler, Gilliam, & Barnett, 2011). Yet evading this debate impedes consideration of organizational features essential to transforming ECE into a competent, coherent field of practice.

## IT CAN BE DONE

Professionalizing ECE is for the purpose of unifying the field as an organized field of practice so individual and collective capacity exists to consistently provide a level of care and education that furthers children's learning and development. This rationale is not unlike what increasingly is being articulated by those questioning current approaches to K–12 reform (Fullan, 2011; Fullan & Hargreaves, 2012; Tucker, 2011). Coherence, consistency, and shared accountability come from well-prepared individuals aligned in common purpose, commitment, and competence in practice, regardless of setting, auspice, or financing source.

Other fields' experiences make evident that attaining attributes associated with professionalism will be gradual, jagged, and ongoing (Brandon & Welch, 2009; The Carnegie Foundation for the Advancement of Teaching, 2010; Dower, O'Neil, & Hough, 2001; Flanagan, 1976; Freidson, 2001; Goffin, 2009). Yet forming ECE as a profession offers a systemic approach for achieving collective competence, creating an alliance between the field's research and practice base, and reducing variability promoted by the absence of professional coherence and by state-by-state and program-by-program differences. Organizing ECE as a profession makes the knowledge and skills associated with competent practice available to all practitioners and to all children.

Transforming ECE as a field of practice will require large dosages of courage, dedication, and stamina. It would be false advertising to suggest otherwise. Yet, our commitment to a different future for ECE and for children and their families can galvanize and sustain us.

"When we speak of choice, what we mean is the ability to exercise control over ourselves and our environment. In order to choose, we must first perceive that control is possible" (Iyengar, 2010, pp. 6–7). Other occupations have pursued professionalism and succeeded; still more are advocating a similar choice. We can, too.

CHAPTER 4

# Moving from Fragmented Connections to a Unified Field of Practice

ECE often confronts the frustrating consequences of its practice fragmentation when grappling with uneven program quality within and across the field's multiple sectors. Forming ECE as a profession can address performance issues by unifying ECE's disjointed expectations for teachers and closing the gap between professed expertise and daily practice.

## ORGANIZING AS A PROFESSION

Professional institutions organize and advance disciplines by overseeing training and certification, and by supporting the creation and refinement of knowledge and skill (Dower, O'Neil, & Hough, 2001; Freidson, 2001; Sullivan, 2005b). As organized fields of preparation and practice, professions address individual capabilities as well as a field's overall capacity to act on its specialized knowledge (Dreeben, 2005; Dower, O'Neil, & Hough, 2001; Freidson, 2001; Sullivan, 2005a, 2005b). Sullivan (2005a, 2005b) highlighted that professions take responsibility for domains of knowledge and skill, generating a social contract between professions and society with strong moral undertones regarding use of this expertise and its management in terms of qualifications, preparation, and oversight.

Use of a field's specialized knowledge—the right to develop, supervise, and evaluate the work, and independence to direct application of developing knowledge—is therefore a fundamental characteristic of professions. This feature forms the basis for structures and institutions that transform a loosely connected field into an *organized* field of preparation and practice: requirements for entry; mandatory credentials; institutions

34

that verify professional practice, such as accreditation and credentialing bodies; proactive organizations that ensure a profession's viability and vitality; and institutions that prepare competent practitioners, most notably institutions of higher education.

These organizational elements are tightly intertwined around mission-driven use of specialized knowledge and skills (Dower, O'Neil, & Hough, 2001; Freidson, 2001). They provide the connective tissue that unifies a field of practice and transforms it into a *system.*

## BECOMING A SYSTEM OF PREPARATION AND PRACTICE

Dictionary definitions of *organized* include "arranged in a systematic way, especially on a large scale" and "functioning within a formal structure, as in the coordination and direction of activities." Examples offered include organized medicine—and my favorite, organized crime!

Reflect for a moment on ECE: It is not systematically arranged in a way that supports fulfillment of a clearly articulated purpose. The field is neither organized around shared intentions nor responsibility for the consequences of its practice. Other than the shared fact of working with children or on their behalf, few commonalities bind the field together in terms of common knowledge, preparation, qualifications, accountability, or aspirations. Rarely do early educators think of their individual roles as part of something larger than their program or its sector.

The absence of an agreed upon name for our field perhaps best exemplifies ECE's fragmented condition. What is the name for this field of practice—early care and education, early education and care, early learning and development (the term chosen by the Race to the Top—Early Learning Challenge), educare, early childhood education, child development? (See Neugebauer, 2008, for more labels.) The possibilities reflect the diversity of opinions on the field's purpose, which in turn is reflected in the range of practices—seen not only in ECE programs but also in training and higher education programs. As Dower, O'Neil, and Hough (2001) stress, "A basic description or definition of the profession in question is primary. Before exploring the details of educational opportunities, regulatory schemes and costs, one needs to know what the profession aims to do" (p. 5).

Professional preparation is the "process of initiating the next generation of practitioners into the several dimensions of the expertise that defines a given profession" (Sullivan, 2005b, p. 207). Specialized expertise is conveyed by a clearly delineated scope of practice, typically accompanied by credentials or degrees (Carnegie Foundation for the Advancement of Teaching, 2010; Dower, O'Neil, & Hough, 2001; Freidson, 2001), that describes the service an individual may provide as well as expertise the practitioner does *not* have (Dower, O'Neil, & Hough, 2001).

## Putting degrees in perspective

Debate has flourished since the National Research Council's 2001 publication of *Eager to Learn* (Bowman, Donovan, Burns, 2001) and its recommendation for early childhood teachers to have bachelor's degrees (e.g., Bogard, Traylor, & Takaishi, 2008; Bueno, Darling-Hammond, & Gonzales, 2010; Early, Bryant, Pianta et al., 2006; Whitebook, 2003; Whitebook & Ryan, 2011; Zigler, Gilliam, & Barnett, 2011). Yet although formally acquired degrees and/or credentials are important to organized fields of practice, degrees and certifications by themselves do not denote professionalism.

Career options often are associated with formal qualifications. Think, for example, of plumbers, electricians, and individuals who work in the worlds of business or technology, none of whom are part of professions, even though their technical expertise makes important contributions to society. Certifications and degrees can convey technical expertise and yet function outside of an organized field of practice.

While requiring four-year degrees of early educators has potential to increase the knowledge and skill of *individual* practitioners—especially when informed by research on child development, curriculum, and effective pedagogy, to advance ECE as a profession, debates about degrees must be placed in the context of a profession's institutional, cultural, and ethical infrastructure.

Variability among degrees and ECE-related credentials in terms of philosophical orientation, content, and clinical experiences, as well as faculty knowledge and skills, obstruct development of collective competence and commitment—nor could it easily be otherwise in the absence of an organized field of practice.[1]

## Professional development systems and professions

Some might counter these points by lifting up state efforts to develop professional development systems and career lattices. Spurred by Wheelock College's 1993 national study of career development in

ECE (Morgan et al., 1993) and by NAEYC's National Institute for Early Childhood Professional Development (Willer & Bredekamp, 1993), the work of building professional development systems and career lattices has been underway for over two decades. Informed by Morgan et al.'s (1993) findings documenting loose connections between training and formal coursework, efforts were initiated to sequence and coordinate disconnected trainings, credentials, and levels of formal preparation.

Simultaneously, NAEYC's National Institute for Early Childhood Professional Development (PDI) set forth to develop a consensually determined articulation of the field's foundational content, with the intent to use this foundation as a platform for identifying the higher order and specialized content associated with different roles (Bredekamp, 1992a; Bredekamp & Willer, 1992; NAEYC, 1994). This aspiration was never fulfilled, however, and professional development system building efforts catalyzed by Wheelock's work proceeded without clarity on the field's purpose or specification of ECE's specialized expertise as a field of practice. Unable to find consensus on these issues, Bredekamp (1992a) concluded, "At this point in our history, the early childhood profession could be viewed as experiencing an identity crisis. We are struggling to define who we are and where we want to go" (p. 54).

Fueled by crossover between the roles of early educators and mothers (Benedict, 1948; Hess, Price, Dickson, & Conroy, 1981; Katz, 1980; Modigliani, 1993; Williams, 1995; Zumwalt, 1984), as well as by its multi-pronged origins, the field's identity issues continually hinder boundary setting. So it should come as no surprise that Huston's preface to the 2012 Institute of Medicine and National Research Council report on the ECE workforce, asserted, "The lack of consensus on a definition of the ECCE work force [referencing early care and education] poses a fundamental challenge"[2] (p. x).

Consequently, professional development efforts and career lattice are remediating disconnected professional development options in the context of diverse statements of purpose and expectations for competence. Reflecting reluctance to entertain differentiated roles and responsibilities or accept credentials and certification as passports for entry into practice (see Bredekamp, 2004; Bredekamp & Willer, 1993; Morgan, 1994a, 1994b), these endeavors rarely link different levels and types of preparation with scopes of practice—nor in the absence of an organized field of practice could this easily be otherwise. As a result, professional development systems emerge state by state, unevenly arranging accessible pathways to training and course work.

## ECE'S HISTORY AS AN ASPIRING PROFESSION

### Historical Antecedents

The field's present professional status can be sourced to its formative history. As historian Finkelstein (1988) pointed out:

> The history and fate of professionalism in early childhood education are inextricably linked to the process of defining childhood education. This process was undertaken in order to raise the status of children and child rearing, mothers and motherhood; to dignify social service; and to solidify the roles of women as moral and cultural authorities and as agents of social control and transformation (pp. 10–11).

As a result, the onset of both Kindergarten and nursery education was based on a voluntary view of work, a gender-linked definition of qualifications and expertise, and missionary zeal (Beatty, 1990; Finkelstein, 1988). As articulated in 1929 by the National Committee on Nursery Schools (which eventually led to the formation of the National Association for Nursery Education, the forerunner of NAEYC) in *Minimum Essentials for Nursery Education*, "Teaching is essentially an art. The ability to teach successfully is sometimes in a person with a minimum of formal training, and no amount of training can be guaranteed to make a good teacher" (no page number).

Then as noted by Cahan (1989), while the expertise surrounding nursery schools came largely from university-based child development researchers, when it came to child care (then labeled day nurseries), it was the field of social work that exerted the greatest influence. Leaping forward in time, even though Head Start's teaching staff increasingly are expected to earn degrees, when founded in 1964 and consistent with the program's then emphasis on community development and individual empowerment, adults from a child's community were preferred, with the intent of supporting community members' upward mobility (Bowman, 2011; Greenberg, 1969).

So, while the field typically assigns responsibility to others for its low stature, our history shows that we've partnered. As Heifetz, Grashow, & Linsky (2009) point out, "The reality is that any social system (including an organization or a country or a family) is the way it is because the people in that system (at least those individuals and factions with the most leverage) want it that way" (p. 17).

## Choices Perpetuating the Field's Fractured Status

As already noted, the strongest underpinning for forming ECE as a profession comes from the nursery school movement/preschools, which is why review of NANE/NAEYC's activities over time provides a window into organizational attempts to form the field as a profession.

Drawing from this historical lineage, ECE has long claimed the mantle of professionalism, and while by almost all indicators the nature of our work aligns with that of a profession, it should now be evident that ECE as a field of practice lacks both the attributes and organization associated with recognized professions: clarity of purpose; organizing structures and supportive institutions that bound practitioners by common knowledge and skills; clear scopes of practice; responsibility for developing and applying a specialized knowledge base; and shared acceptance of ethical responsibility to perform at a level of competence capable of consistently promoting children's learning and development.

NAEYC's Conceptual Framework for Early Childhood Professional Development (1994) illustrates the distinction I have labored to explain and the disparity between the field's present development efforts and the work of forming ECE as a profession. "The lattice (versus ladder) distinguishes *the early childhood field* from the *early childhood profession*. The *field* includes anyone engaged in the provision of early childhood services; the *profession* denotes those who have acquired some professional knowledge and are on a professional path" (p. 71, emphasis in original).

A professional path is defined as (1) completion of or enrollment in a credit-bearing early childhood professional preparation program or (2) ongoing participation in formal training that may not be credit-bearing but will lead to increased competency that can be formally assessed (p. 71). As concisely characterized by Morgan (1994b): "A professional is anyone who is working with young children and/or their parents and who is on a professional path toward commitment and further learning" (p. 12).

Described as a new paradigm for professional development (NAEYC, 1994; Willer & Bredekamp, 1993), this model incorporated VanderVen's (1988) conceptualization of professionalization as the degree to which a field is advancing toward meeting recognized criteria for a profession. It focuses on "the process of professionalizing rather than on defining the product 'professional'" (Willer & Bredekamp, 1993, p. 64).

The position taken by *ECE for a New Era* differs substantively from the "in process" definition advanced by NAEYC's Conceptual Framework.

Yet one cannot but be in awe of the conceptual leadership represented by the papers developed as part of NAEYC's Professional Development Institute (1993). Further, in light of feared losses and engrained habits of mind, the reasoning becomes more apparent. As expressed at the time by Bredekamp (1992b), "It probably wasn't Winston Churchill, but somebody said, 'We are our own worst enemies.' The barrier of attitudes among early childhood professionals seems to be the hardest to talk about, the most divisive, and perhaps the one that most strongly thwarts our efforts for change" (p. 38).

While these choices foiled formation of ECE as a profession, they provided a framework for moving the field forward.[3] Yet 20-plus years later, the same issues remain unresolved and lack of competent teachers increasingly is recognized as the field's core dilemma. The time has come for choices of the 1990s to be revisited and for the field to address its longstanding gridlock.

ECE has seen dramatic changes since the 1990s. Beyond societal changes and a more demanding political context, research studies document the field's inadequate performance, even as the knowledge base for informing effective practice has expanded. It is more possible than in the past to prepare skilled ECE teachers and thus more erroneous to ignore what is known.

## AN ORGANIZATIONAL OPTION FOR ECE
## AS A PROFESSION

### Making Hard Choices

Then there is the fact that provision of ECE programs has become more complex and increasingly reliant on an expanding and multi-faceted knowledge base, making it more difficult to rely solely on program standards to improve children's formal learning experiences. Absent consistent standards for individuals, reliance on program standards, typically in association with discrete federal and state funding policies, adds to the field's fragmentation, generating inconsistencies in quality and uneven results across programs (Bredekamp & Goffin, 2012).

Now well into the 21st century, others are making choices on the field's behalf, choices often detached from the field's knowledge base and accumulated practical wisdom. While forces external to ECE will always play a role in shaping its future, the question at hand is the extent to which ECE is prepared to be part of these advancements—not only as individual advocates but as an organized field of practice.

ECE needs to determine if and how it wants to respond to its current reality. The status quo can be maintained—which, we must acknowledge, represents a choice—and responsibility can be delegated to others to "formulate, distribute, and supervise" the field's work (Freidson, 2001, p. 50). If the field chooses to continue on its present track, it could consider augmenting the field's existing professional development framework by encouraging practitioners to act in ways aligned with the tenets of professionalism (Feeney, 2012). This approach, however, maintains professional-like behavior as an individual choice. Alternatively, ECE can choose to move beyond the limitations of conceptualizing professionalism solely as an individual "in-process" undertaking, engage with the difficulties inherent to defining the "product 'professional,'" and become a recognized profession with its benefits and obligations.

Most of us in this field are passionate about the work we do. We consistently express a desire for ECE to provide the very best learning and development experiences for children and for its practitioners to be acknowledged as professionals. The field's present status is the result of differing purposes and choice avoidance, not ill intent. Yet too many children are denied the benefits of good ECE programs—not only because of insufficient financing and disconnected policies but because of the field's reluctance to assume responsibility for its collective competence.

By organizing as a profession, the field can circumvent limits established by funding standards and provide a coherent framework for public policy. Professions advance their fields of practice by upgrading every practitioner's competence, regardless of setting, program sponsor, or source of financing. Forming ECE as a profession can make it possible for every child to encounter a good teacher.

Collective competence depends on consistently well-prepared individuals instilled with commitment to continuous learning. Growing attention to responsive teacher-child interactions and effective instruction plus explosive growth in mentoring and coaching indicate that the importance of "individual quality" finally is being acknowledged. Yet as long as these efforts reside outside of an organized field of practice bound by clarity of purpose and responsibility, their impact will be uneven, succeeding in improving the practice of some teachers but omitting others. "We can't avoid the fact that any choice we make may be considered a statement about who we are, but some choices speak more loudly than others. . . . The less a choice serves some utilitarian function, the more it implies about identity" (Iyengar, 2010, p. 103).

## ECE's Expertise as a Field of Practice

Never has more been expected of ECE's teachers. While improving program quality seldom is omitted from discussions on ECE, only recently has improving the practice of early educators been elevated as an intervention strategy[4] (Kagan, Kauerz, & Tarrant, 2008; IOM & NRC, 2012; U.S. Department of Education & U.S. Department of Health and Human Services, 2011; Whitebook, 2010).

Developmentally appropriate practice applied in the context of meaningful interactions with teachers, peers, and intellectually interesting curriculum has been a defining practice and value almost since the field's inception (Copple & Bredekamp, 2009; Goffin, 2001). Given that subject matter knowledge is the province of other specialists (such as mathematicians, scientists, and so forth), Lortie (1969) suggested that pedagogy represented the unique expertise of teachers (p. 24).

Developmentally appropriate practice coincides with what Schulman (2005) calls a profession's signature pedagogy. While tightly intertwined with the content being shared and learning being facilitated, developmentally effective pedagogy provides a starting place for conceptualizing the specialized expertise of ECE as a professional field of practice.

According to Schulman (2005), a signature pedagogy offers a window into a field's personality, disposition, and culture, and professions are more likely than other academic disciplines to have them.

> Professional education is not education for understanding alone; it is preparation for accomplished and responsible practice in the service of others. It is preparation for "good work." Professionals must learn abundant amounts of theory and vast bodies of knowledge. They must come to understand in order to act, and they must act in order to serve (p. 53).

Embedded in this quote are three fundamental dimensions of professional work: "to *think*, to *perform*, and to *act with integrity*" (p. 52, emphasis in original).[5] As I hope is now evident, of these three dimensions, ECE is least developed in the area of performance and its union with "think" and "act with integrity." Some attention has been given to the "think" part of this trio, typically defined as teachers' purposeful decision making (Bredekamp, 2011; Copple & Bredekamp, 2009; Katz, 1984). And although acting with integrity, that is, adhering to an ethical code, is a personal choice rather than a collective responsibility, multiple codes of ethics are available to early educators, with the code promulgated by NAEYC probably best known (Feeney, 2012).

All three of these dimensions are uneven in expression however; so considerable development work awaits us. Yet, in conjunction with research on effective practice, the fundamentals for thinking, performing, and acting with integrity are available for undergirding ECE as a profession. Once ECE's purpose is defined, professional boundaries are drawn, and pre-requisite knowledge and skills are determined, these fundamentals can be woven together into a system of thinking, performing, and acting that binds ECE as an organized field of practice.

## A Conversation Starter: ECE as a Profession of Subfields

*ECE for a New Era* argues for parting ways with ECE's habits of mind and stepping forward together to construct ECE's future as a professional field of practice. Unifying ECE is made more difficult, however, by an operating assumption that each of the field's sectors—Head Start, preschool/Pre-K (some would see these as distinctive), early intervention/early childhood special education, and various forms of child care—has the same intentions for its interactions with children and families. As articulated by NAEYC's Conceptual Framework for Early Childhood Professional Development (NAEYC, 1994), despite differences in funding and regulatory agencies, "the service varies little when done in an appropriate manner for an individual child" (p. 70).

Although now archived as a position statement, NAEYC's Conceptual Framework continues to inform the field's professional development efforts. Concentrating on children's similarities impedes attention to variations in programs' intentions and, pragmatically, requires surmounting complications resulting from differences in policy rationales, regulations, financial support, occupational identities, and public expectations.

*Ready or Not* (Goffin & Washington, 2007) questioned whether ECE should continue viewing itself as an undifferentiated field of endeavor or, instead, organize as a field comprised of subfields.[6] Like nursing and other fields in health care, ECE as a field of practice might be comprised of organized subfields or specialties characterized by distinctive scopes of practice and unique contributions to children's early learning and development—yet bound together by a common overarching purpose, expert body of knowledge, and shared professional identity.

Even though NAEYC's 1994 Conceptual Framework focused on improving ECE through an individual process of professionalizing, it still assigned ECE as a field of practice the responsibility for distinguishing it from other professions.

> A defining characteristic of any profession is a specialized body of knowledge and competencies shared by all of its members that are not shared by others. ... Does every childhood professional need to know and be able to do this in order to effectively practice? ... Does the sum of this body of knowledge and competencies uniquely distinguish the early childhood professional from all other professionals? (p. 72)

An expert body of knowledge and competencies unifies a profession's thinking, performing, and ethical behaviors. Specializations are delineated by their relationship to other bodies of knowledge (Freidson, 2001). If ECE wants to be a freestanding profession—versus, for example, a specialty within a broader field such as education or family support—at least two specialties will need to come together to form the whole.

So beyond ECE's shared expert body of knowledge and competencies, additional, and unique, expectations could exist for what practitioners should know and be able to do, depending on the ECE program, its purpose, ages of children served and/or results expected from practitioners—or some defensible combination of these or other variables—resulting in a subset of specialized knowledge and skills. Think, for example, of the distinction between occupational and physical therapists. This differentiation is what provides the basis for a *scope of practice*, describing what falls within as well as outside the range of one's expertise (American Nurses Association, 2010; Dower, O'Neil, & Hough, 2001).

Only a limited stretch in thinking seems needed to appreciate that teacher-child and family interactions within early intervention programs such as Head Start are different from that in child care; that early childhood special education requires knowledge and expertise over and beyond what Pre-K teachers of typically developing children need to know and be able to do; that Early Head Start programs place demands on child development specialists not experienced by caregivers in child care settings serving the same age group.[7]

Although teachers in these settings have specialized knowledge and skills in common, and a shared goal of preparing children developmentally and educationally, their approach for promoting this result varies by the program's specialized purpose and the target population being served—as does their need for specialized knowledge and skills. Well-developed answers to the "who," "what," "where," "when," and "how" associated with scopes of practice, including boundaries and membership, can be used to provide a complete picture of individual subfields.

Nursing specializations are defined by education, experience, role, and population served (see Figure 4.1). Nursing standards delineate practitioner responsibilities (American Nurses Association, 2004). "Written in measureable terms, standards also define the nursing profession's accountability to the public and the outcomes for which registered nurses are responsible" (American Nurses Association, 2004, p. 1).

Will this approach prioritize or privilege one role as more important than another? The answer should be "no" if each role is associated with a well-defined scope of practice and preparation. While they may differ in amount and kind of preparation, scope of practice, and extent of

**Figure 4.1. Criteria for Nursing Specialties**

A nursing specialty:
1. Defines itself as nursing.
2. Is clearly defined.
3. Has a well derived knowledge base particular to the practice of the nursing specialty.
4. Is concerned with phenomena of the discipline of nursing.
5. Subscribes to the overall purposes and functions of nursing.
6. Can identify a need and demand for itself.
7. Adheres to the overall licensure, certification, and education requirements of the profession.
8. Defines competencies for the area of specialty nursing practice.
9. Has existing mechanisms for supporting, reviewing, and disseminating research to support its knowledge base and evidence-based practice.
10. Has defined educational criteria for specialty preparation or graduate degree.
11. Has continuing education programs or other mechanisms for nurses in the specialty to maintain competence.
12. Is practiced nationally or internationally.
13. Includes a substantial number of registered nurses who devote most of their professional time to the specialty.
14. Is organized and represented by a national or international specialty association or branch of a parent organization.

*Source:* American Nurses Association, 2010.

responsibility, each role can and should be recognized for contributing to children's early learning.

While organizing into subfields may seem radical in the context of ECE, for other professions, it is commonplace. Maintaining good health, for example, depends on access to internists and surgeons or on interactions with a nurse anesthetist as well as a practical nurse. Competence relies on differentiated skills and preparation; yet each builds on a common knowledge base.

Although not absent philosophical and practical intricacies, organizing ECE as a profession of subfields responds to many of the field's concerns about professionalism. It also shifts attention from program performance to individual competence. It opens possibilities for rethinking relationships between and among programs, offers the prospect of differential amounts and kinds of preparation, and suggests a more nuanced framework for tackling the issue of compensation. Signaling the intuitive validity of this approach, three states mandate that Pre-K programs operate at levels three through five in their QRISs: Vermont, Pennsylvania, and North Carolina (Office of Planning, Research, and Evaluation, 2010), tacitly acknowledging that different expectations and requirements coexist for teachers in different types of ECE programs. ECE also has national "specialty" organizations such as the National Head Start Association, Association of Family Child Care, and Division for Early Childhood of the Council for Exceptional Children, indicating that these sectors view themselves as having specialized knowledge and interests that warrant a separate association.

While some may contend this approach would add additional complexity to an already splintered field, it could be argued that it might instead simplify the field's system building efforts by:

- Identifying direct interactions with children focused on teaching with educational and developmental intentions as the defining core of the field's work.
- Unifying the field's multiple strands around a shared, overarching purpose;
- Dissolving the schism between "care" and "education";
- Bringing clarity and consistency to ECE's work within sectors;
- Embracing the field's disparate histories and occupational identities;
- Acknowledging differences in competencies needed by various teaching roles as well as by support roles outside the classroom/ provider program setting; and

- Creating a system better able to accommodate differences between market-based and government-funded programs.

The possibility of ECE as a profession of subfields is offered as a conversation starter. It is hoped it will catalyze exploration of its merits plus still other possibilities. The *Next Steps Commentaries* that follow Chapter 5 offer additional conversation starters. As Iyengar (2010) reminds us, "To choose means to turn ourselves to the future" (p. 260).

# CHAPTER 5

# Stepping Forward Together

> Occasionally something different happens, a collective awakening to
> new possibilities that changes *everything* over time. (Senge et al., 2010,
> p. 5, emphasis in original)

ECE has undergone dramatic changes since the 1960s. It has become recognized as having singular potential for enhancing children's developmental and educational trajectories, especially when they are developmentally at risk. Seeking to maximize ECE's potential, policymakers, business leaders, and philanthropists have applied their resources and influence to form ECE as a field of practice. And after years of focused research, ECE's clinical knowledge base is informing evidence-based practice.

Early educators' crucial role in effecting positive learning and development is now empirically confirmed. No longer is it possible to ignore consequences stemming from inconsistencies in practitioners' knowledge and skills. Further, escalating expectations for accountability have politicized the stakes; so much so that Pianta (2012) asserted, "Performance accountability is a tectonic shift in regulating ECCE [referring to early care and education]–and fundamentally tied to the idea that human capital is quality" (p. 27).

Acknowledging its changing context, in the 1990s the field started conceptualizing and engaging with system building activities, identifying gaps in state and federal policies and striving for policy, structural, and procedural alignment to improve programs and services. Fullan (2011), however, has argued that these change strategies, while having a role in education's "reform constellation" (p. 6), are ineffective for tackling whole system reform because they "alter structure, procedures and other formal attributes of the system without reaching the internal substance of reform" (p. 5).

Organizing ECE as a professional field of practice tackles the "internal substance of reform": Once ECE coheres as a field of practice, there will at last be a focal point for program alignment, coordination of policies and regulations, and continuous improvement.

# PROFESSIONALISM AS A FIELD-UNIFYING STRATEGY

*ECE for a New Era* makes three claims: (1) ECE as a field of practice should take responsibility for the competent practice of its practitioners and for facilitating positive consequences for children's learning and development; (2) ECE should formally organize as a profession to develop collective competence and realize consistency in practice across sites and program types; (3) ECE should develop fieldwide leadership, shrinking its reliance on public policy for *defining* its purpose and structure, thereby addressing a dependency that has fostered programmatic and systemic fragmentation, uneven performance, and weak leadership capacity as a field of practice.

The field recognizes the need to improve its overall level of practice, generating strategies such as Quality Rating and Improvement Systems (QRIS). Increasingly viewed as an accountability tool tied to children's school readiness (Zellman & Karoly, 2012), QRISs have evolved during their decade-plus of existence into a proposed field-unifying strategy with strong federal backing. Yet, emerging research, variation across states, and implementation challenges are prompting questions about its ability to serve as an effective field-unifying strategy.

Drawing from positive experiences in other countries, Kagan (2012) offers another option: states' early learning standards. She proposes that early learning standards are under-utilized for coalescing ECE around what children need to know and be able to do and for driving pedagogical and curricular reform. Confounded, however, by the field's internal divisions, state contexts, and policy variations, states' early learning standards vary widely, including the extent to which states' early learning standards are informed by research (Scott-Little, Kagan, & Frelow, 2006), further fueling internal variability.

Organizing ECE as a professional field of practice is presented as a third, more encompassing field-unifying option. While not absent shortcomings, forming ECE as a profession is the only one that:

- Relies on self-determination.
- Reduces ECE's internal fragmentation by systematizing it as a field of preparation and practice.
- Requires the field's practice to be accountable to professionally developed standards based on ECE's specialized knowledge.
- Supports ongoing, continuous improvement by building fieldwide leadership and shared obligation to competent practice.

- Creates a system that can foster coherent policy support.
- Lessens the field's entanglements with external politics, recently exemplified by Missouri legislators' 2012 decision to prohibit QRIS by law.

Repercussions from not stepping forward and exercising fieldwide leadership to unify ECE as a field of practice already are apparent: Concerned leaders external to ECE, including policymakers, are progressively becoming more active in making decisions on the field's behalf in order to redress children's uneven preparation for Kindergarten.

The field's future is embedded in the present (Drucker, 2003; Naisbett, 2006). Unless we step forward, ECE's evolving purpose and fate will likely diverge from historic values and future aspirations.

To be clear: I am *not* suggesting that ECE on its own can—or should—transform and sustain itself as a field of practice. Rather, I am accentuating that ECE is absent as an *organized field of practice* in this defining moment when key decisions are dictating its practice and structure. We have yet to step forward to assume responsibility and accountability for the practice of early childhood education.

## STEPPING UP TO THE CHALLENGE

This final chapter outlines four discrete yet interwoven activities for getting unstuck[1] and creating change: altering our individual mindsets; recognizing ECE's systemic attitudes and behaviors; coming together to reach consensus on next steps; and building leadership capacity. While not all the steps involved in mobilizing and creating change,[2] they provide formative starting points.

Forming ECE as a profession will be neither swift nor easy. As should be expected from a tough challenge, it will be a journey with twists and unexpected turns. Participants on similar journeys relay that actions and decisions typically emerge while engaged with the work, precluding development of a detailed or long-term blueprint. Co-creating a future that transforms "what is" requires experimentation and perseverance (Heifetz, Grashow, & Linsky, 2009; Senge et al., 2005, 2010; Kahane, 2010, 2012). "Like others before you," Senge et al. (2010) prophesized, "you will discover much of the plot as you invent it" (p. 141).

The necessity of implementing choices that involve loss defines this work as adaptive. The presence of dynamic, social, and generative complexity identifies it as a tough challenge. The chance to move beyond problem solving to forge a new direction marks it as a transformative opportunity.

Kahane (2012) shared the following from a participant in a complex social change initiative: "If we keep repeating the same stories about our country, then we will keep doing the same things, which do not work. But we are addicted to this repetition! We need to get fed up with these same stories. We need new stories" (p. 90).

It's disconcerting to realize how easily this quote could be rewritten with "ECE" as a substitution for "country." If the field chooses, though, this can be the moment in time when ECE moves beyond its current narrative and creates a new scenario for its future.

## Changing Ourselves So We Can Change Together

The field's problematic situation has been identified: ECE is underperforming as a field of practice, and many of us no longer are comfortable continuing as is. By choosing to come together and being open to change, we can respond to the adaptive challenges around purpose and responsibility and create a new storyline for ECE as a professional field of practice.

Each of us has contributed to the system we now wish to change; we each own a piece of the problem we're trying to address. Each of us, therefore, will have to step back to step forward—to consider how our thoughts and behaviors are contributing, however inadvertently, to the status quo.

Bringing about and sustaining whole system reform is unlikely without changes in individual behaviors and altering beliefs giving rise to these behaviors (Heifetz, Grashow, & Linsky, 2009; Kegan & Lahey, 2001; Senge et al., 2010). If we are to be successful at changing together, we first must be open to changing ourselves.

Stepping forward in this way means asking questions such as: "What as individuals are we doing or not doing that prevents our commitment to ECE as a profession from being fully realized? What might be lost—what might we as individuals lose—if we acted on the opportunity to organize as a profession? What am I avoiding?" (adapted from Kegan & Lahey, 2001). Questions such as these challenge us to explore assumptions that may be blocking us from considering different possibilities.

"They are not so much the assumptions we have," contend Kegan and Lahey, "as they are assumptions *that have us*" (p. 83, emphasis in original). These assumptions maintain the status quo by:

- Appearing automatically without intention or awareness,
- Being viewed as truths,
- Creating a sense of certainty that our worldview is reality, and
- Anchoring and sustaining our equilibrium (p. 86).

Since disrupting one's equilibrium is uncomfortable, we tend to avoid it. Yet change starts with us—not with someone else. Changes in thinking can open up different ways of imagining ECE and its options. Genuinely considering questions such as those listed in Figure 5.1 can alter our individual relationship to change, making it possible to explore these questions with others and together imagine differently.

### Figure 5.1. Questions to Ask of Ourselves and Each Other

1. What assumptions am I making that may be influencing how I'm hearing/responding to another's ideas?
2. What's holding me/us back from changing? From changing the field's status quo? What am I/are we afraid of?
3. To what or whom am I being loyal? Who would react most strongly if I did something differently? Is this preventing me/us from change?
4. What triggers my/our "buttons"?
5. What limits are self-imposed versus driven by external forces?
6. What would happen if an assumption turned out to be wrong?
7. If we had all of the money we needed, what would we still need to do?
8. What obstacles to change could be removed or reduced to create space for innovation and change?
9. Will my/our ideas promote fundamental change or are they more of a quick fix solution?
10. Who will be affected by a proposed idea? How will they be affected?
11. Is my thinking/our conversation anchored in the future or in the past?
12. Am I/Are we abandoning what really is wanted in order to avoid anxiety or stress?
13. Am I/Are we focused on achieving what we want or being "less bad"?
14. What am I/are we doing—or not doing—that prevents becoming a profession from being fully realized?

*Source:* Drawn from Heifetz, Grashow, & Linsky (2009); Kahane (2012); Kegan & Lahey (2001); Senge et al. (2010).

## Recognizing ECE's Systemic Attitudes and Behaviors

Creating a new storyline will require the field to recognize its systemic attitudes and behaviors. To assist with identifying systemic obstacles, ten system archetypes have been identified (Herasymowych & Senko, 2012; Senge, 1990). Representing generic, repetitive patterns of behavior, archetypes describe complex systems from the perspective of what's not working and offer potential change strategies. They function as diagnostic tools for identifying the forces governing a particular system—for understanding one's current story.

Recall the field's four habits of mind identified in Chapter 2: Timidity as a field of practice; resistance to distinctive scopes of practice; an evangelical orientation; and dependency on others to advance the field's merit. These habits of mind correspond to three systems archetypes: *Attractiveness Principle, Drifting Goals,* and *Shifting the Burden* (see Systems Archetypes box).

Systems archetypes were developed to facilitate problem solving—to spur deeper thinking about attitudes and behaviors hindering change. Since then, Herasymowych and Senko (2012) have conceptually inverted them to identify attitudes and behaviors needed to propel systemic change.

The *Attractiveness Principle* is reframed as *Be Your Best:* "We have boundaries of what we can and cannot do." *Drifting Goals* is recast as *Stay on Track* and described as "We monitor, evaluate, and adjust performance standards in order to achieve our goals." *Shifting the Burden* is reorganized as *Bite the Bullet:* "We are willing and able to invest the time and effort required to implement the fundamental solution" (pp. 7–8).

Importantly, the mental models associated with each archetype also change.

---

### Systems Archetypes Applicable to ECE
### as a Field of Practice

---

*Attractiveness Principle:* We are trying to be all things to all people.

*Drifting Goals:* We have lowered our standards to close the gap between the actual and desired performance.

*Shifting the Burden:* We know the fundamental solution, but are unwilling or unable to take it; so we implement a symptomatic solution and deal with the side effects.

---

*Source:* Herasymowych & Senko, 2012; Senge, 1990

- The *Attractiveness Principle* changes *from* "We must please everyone all of the time." *to* "We cannot please everybody."
- *Drifting Goals* changes *from* "Our current level of activity is acceptable, even though it is below standard." *to* "We know where we are going and what it will take to get there."
- *Shifting the Burden* changes *from* "We know what to do, but it's too difficult to deal with; so let's put on a bandage instead." *to* "We take responsibility and spend the time and effort required to be effective, even if it's difficult" (pp. 6–8).

Note the repeated use of the plural pronoun "we." While reliant on change in individual attitudes and behaviors, systemic change requires collective thinking and action. Revising the field's systemic mindsets can reduce barriers to change and invigorate action, making ECE's transformation more doable (see Table 5.1).

## Convening a Microcosm of the Field[3]

Bringing together a microcosm of the field is for the purpose of exploring different organizational structures for ECE as a profession, achieving consensus, and deciding how to move forward.

It begins by engaging a team of people from across ECE who are capable of influencing the system's future (Kahane, 2012; Senge et al., 2005, 2010). Based on their experiences, Senge et al. (2005) start with people "who could be the change" (p. 151), choosing individuals with commitment, passion, and experience with change rather than positions on an organizational chart.

Ensuring the system's parts are represented is key. So it's possible to delve deeply into issues and co-create alternatives for organizing as a profession, the stakeholder leadership group should not be too large. For these gatherings to ultimately influence change, though, a strategy also has to be developed for engaging broadly with others to transform the system (Kahane, 2012; Senge et al., 2010).

Kahane (2012) recommends an initial group of five to ten individuals who, in turn, build a whole system team of 25–35 well-respected individuals to create options for moving forward—a process involving intense questioning and learning so shared understanding of the overall system is developed and a feasible plan of action can emerge.

Recall that this process involves toggling between adaptation and transformation. So, these conversations should focus on what *could* be

**Table 5.1. Systemic Dispositions for Action**

| Instead of | Positive Archetype* | Mental Model/Mindset* |
|---|---|---|
| Timidity as a field of practice | Bite the bullet | Take responsibility and apply the time and effort required to be effective, even if it's difficult. |
| Resistance to distinctive scopes of practice & an evangelical orientation | Be our best | Not everybody can be pleased. |
| Dependency on others to advance the field's merit | Stay on track | We know where we want to go and what it takes to get there. |

*Adapted from Herasymowych & Senko, 2012, pp. 7–8

achieved, not what any one of us individually may wish (Kahane, 2012). Even as it engages with creating a different future, the field's realities have to be considered.

This dynamic hinges on the relationship between creative and emotional tension. Creative tension emerges from the gap between what we want to see exist in the world and the world as it exists. This tension can be resolved in one of two ways: Pulling the vision down toward reality or pulling reality toward the vision (Senge et al., 2010).

Inevitably, creative tension generates emotional tension: fears, anxieties, anger, sadness and more that accompany efforts to close gaps between a vision and the current reality (Heifetz, 1994; Senge et al., 2010). Lowering our goals to be closer to current reality can reduce this emotional tension. Yet by doing so, we risk "destroying what we are trying to nurture" (Kahane, 2010, p. 47).

Fieldwide leadership (discussed below) helps manage these tensions by providing a holding environment. *Holding environments*, sometimes called *containers*, refer to the properties of a relationship that keep people engaged with one another despite divisive forces associated with the work (Heifetz, Grashow, & Linsky, 2009; Kahane, 2010, 2012; Senge et al., 2010; Stookey, 2003).

## Changing Together Through Individual and Fieldwide Leadership

Responding to the challenges of adaptive, systemic, and transformational change requires individual and collective leadership capacity dispersed throughout the ECE field and system. This capacity is expressed to the degree that the system is functioning effectively (Ubels, Fowler, & Acquaye-Baddoo, 2010). Yet perhaps because of the concentration on advocacy to propel fieldwide change, limited attention has been given to developing other forms of individual and collective leadership.

***Individual leadership.*** The field regularly alludes to the importance of individual leadership, but in practice it receives minimal consideration. To quote Bowman and Kagan (1997),

> The early care and education field historically has approached leadership as something that happens to some people. Until recently, we have not tended to accord it the serious analysis and action that it deserves. This is true at practical and conceptual levels. We have underestimated the importance of leadership to the advancement of the field and the children and families served. Moreover, we have been unclear about what is meant by leadership and where it can and should exist. (p. 157)

Notwithstanding Bowman and Kagan's suggestion in 1997 that the issue of leadership was gaining attention, it has remained a low priority. Surveys in 2009 and 2013 of ECE leadership development programs (Goffin & Means, 2009; Goffin & Janke, 2013) revealed the limited number of programs providing individuals with the knowledge and skills associated with effective leadership.

Additionally, change leadership increasingly is associated with groups, institutions, communities, and networks (Senge et al., 2005, 2010). Consequently, enhancing the leadership capacity of ECE's infrastructure—inclusive of government, nonprofit and for-profit organizations—is essential to strengthening ECE's effectiveness. While it exceeds the scope of *ECE for a New Era* to delve into leadership topics and approaches, the box titled "Leadership Principles" identifies principles pertinent to systemic, adaptive, and transformational change.

***Fieldwide leadership.*** Moving forward as a professionally competent field of practice requires not only individual and institutional leadership but also fieldwide leadership–leadership focused on advancing fields of practice to higher levels of capability (Dower, O'Neil, & Hough, 2001; Goffin, 2009; Rhodes & Huston, 2012). According to Dower, O'Neil, and Hough (2001), "The ability of a profession to understand and adapt to change is an indication of its viability. A profession's role in leading positive change is an indication of its strength" (p. 20).

Numerous colleagues have been asked who they would suggest carry out the fieldwide work outlined in *Ready or Not* and *ECE for a New Era*. Typically, after an extended pause and sometimes a verbal walk-through of prominent organizations, the answer has been, "That's an interesting question. I don't know" (p. 1).

Although not using the terminology of fieldwide leadership, others have noted its absence as well. As mentioned in an earlier chapter, Weber (1969) lamented its absence when Kindergartens were being reformed in the 1960s. Summarizing the field's leadership needs in the late 1990s, Bowman and Kagan (1997) concluded, "professional organizations must take an instrumental role in promoting change in the field" (p. 157).

But when analyzing findings from a cross-occupational examination of entry standards, preparation systems, and individual credentialing

---

### Leadership Principles Associated with Adaptive, Systemic, and Transformational Change

Leadership:

- Is an activity rather than a role–emphasis should be placed on exercising leadership vs. only on individuals in particular roles.
- Is not reliant on authority. It can be exercised by anyone, although typically leadership relies on a high level of personal development.
- Is relationship- and context-based.
- Requires suspending preconceived ideas.
- Necessitates consideration of multiple perspectives.
- Relies on collaboration across boundaries.
- Means "stepping forward" and mobilizing others to join in.
- Involves experimentation, continual diagnosis of what is occurring, and living with uncertainty.
- Embraces learning, adapting, creating, and responds to emerging possibilities.
- Entails choices.
- Requires courage.
- Demands perseverance.

practices of various occupations, Mitchell (1996) noted that in ECE, "There is no one professional organization that unites the preschool-child care occupations across all roles and settings. Instead, there are a number of what might be called role-related professional organizations." Mitchell then added, "The primary characteristic of all of these organizations is that the vast majority of their members are the people who work in these particular sectors or roles. Their organizational missions are to support their members in their roles, provide peer support, and otherwise represent their members' concerns" (p. 113).

In contrast, fieldwide leadership attends to an entire field of practice. As described by Merton (1958), it "is a kind of organizational gadfly, stinging the profession into new and more demanding formulations of purpose" (p. 52). Research by Goffin (2009) found it to be:

- Inwardly focused on the field's need to change or advance its practice;
- Directed toward transforming a discipline as a field of practice;
- Focused on moving an overall field forward as a more viable, coherent, accountable, and respected field of practice; and
- Typically systemic, adaptive, and/or transformative in nature.

Seeking insight into ECE's apparent fieldwide leadership void, Goffin (2009) explored whether and how other fields of practice (nursing, social work, financial planning, opportunity finance [comprised of community development financial institutions], and quality management) exercised leadership related to issues of fieldwide significance that required broad involvement. Field-leading organizations held in common three interlocking traits:

- They were well-defined membership organizations.
- They provided "holding environments" for the work of fieldwide change, making it possible for participants to stay engaged despite the turbulence.
- They were sensitive to the field's context and were future and action oriented (p. 33).

Change and adapting to new realities were consistent themes, with the intent of identifying what was necessary to maintain and/or advance the field as a whole and ensure that members could competently respond to what would be expected of them in the future.

It follows that internal change efforts typically focused on improving practice. Each field-leading organization saw its vision being achieved through members' enhanced performance and by restructuring the context for their work. The former provided the impetus for exercising internal leadership, and the latter provided the focus for advocacy and policy activities. Throughout, these fieldwide organizations consciously and proactively attended to issues associated with their field's unity and collective competence (Goffin, 2009).

To lead for its future, ECE needs a leadership infrastructure. A long-range perspective enabled by fieldwide leadership in combination with diverse forms of individual and organizational leadership can re-set ECE's developmental trajectory and the future it wants to foster for young children.

This is a defining moment. ECE is in the midst of transition as a field of practice. Chapter 2 suggested that the field was in a developmental phase of *Systems Building and Self-Realization*. To be determined is the extent to which ECE will choose to lead for its future and advance toward self-realization.

It's up to each of us, individually and collectively, to step forward. The decision is ours to make.

# Next Steps:
# Three Commentaries

The commentaries that follow offer three viewpoints on forming ECE as a professional field of practice, including proposals for next steps. The three authors–Jacqueline Jones, Rolf Grafwallner, and Pamela J. Winton–bring different backgrounds, expertise, and ideas on ECE as a field of practice. Jacqueline argues that the field needs to step up to the opportunity to define itself as a field of practice and proposes as a catalyst a field-led Council on Early Childhood Education. Rolf focuses on the importance of unifying preparation of the child care and education sectors and suggests a progressive, laddered credentialing system. Looking to implementation science, Pam identifies actions the field can take to enter into the work of organizing ECE as a system of preparation and practice even as she worries about the "devils in the details." These three commentaries offer additional perspectives on how we might engage in organizing ECE as a profession.

---

PUBLIC POLICY AND ECE:
WHO SHOULD DEFINE THE PROFESSION?

*Jacqueline Jones*

---

Goffin's call to professionalize the field of early childhood education (ECE) comes at an important policy moment. Thirty-nine states now support ECE (Barnett, Carolan, Fitzgerald, & Squires, 2011), but with multiple sets of program standards, varying degrees of quality, and ultimately varying levels of impact on young children's success in school.

In the Obama Administration's first term the U.S. Department of Education put a new focus on *early learning* with almost a billion new dollars from programs such as the Race to the Top-Early Learning Challenge, Promise Neighborhoods, and the i3 competition. The effectiveness of state and federal ECE programs and policies in closing the achievement gap at

Kindergarten entry and beyond will depend upon strong leadership from the ECE field, leadership that can work in partnership with policymakers.

Opportunities for increased state and federal investments in ECE make this a timely moment for the ECE community to engage in self-reflection to respond to difficult questions: Who is an ECE professional? Who should set and monitor the standards and expectations for children, early childhood educators, and ECE programs? What constitutes accountability for ECE professionals and programs? Where does ECE fit within the larger context of the country's K–12 education system?

## Needed: A Shared Set of Principles

Three experiences shape my thinking on where we are as a field of practice: (1) as an educational researcher investigating issues in early childhood assessment, (2) as a state official implementing a state-funded preschool program, and (3) as a federal official leading the design of an interagency early learning agenda within the U.S. Department of Education.

From each vantage point the ECE field appears to be a complex and overlapping assortment of stakeholders defined by funding streams, children's age levels, issues associated with ethnicity and language, income, service settings, and so forth, plus the voices of smart, committed individuals fighting for higher program quality and increased access as seen through their particular lenses.

The recent focus on systemic impact requires deep understanding of this complex landscape. However, state and federal policymakers must make decisions quickly and hope that the funding and regulatory authority they hold will be used wisely and will make meaningful changes in the lives of young children. But even well-intentioned policymakers cannot be attuned to every nuance of the ECE field; they must rely on input from the field. Yet, given the field's fragmentation, this typically results in those multiple perspectives noted above working individually to influence policy. When the ECE field cannot present a shared view on core beliefs, policymakers craft policy without input from the field, respond to the most persistent voice, or do nothing.

While absolute agreement on every issue is not possible or productive in any profession or field of study, a set of core beliefs should exist that tie members together and defines the field as a profession. I propose that it is not the role of state and federal policymakers to define ECE's core beliefs. Rather, policy should support a set of core beliefs defined by the profession.

## Beginning a New Conversation

Shortly before President Obama's first term, Kagan and Reid (2008) proposed five functions for the federal government regarding ECE. The first two are noteworthy for this discussion:

- "Provide the *coordinated long-term vision and leadership* for the development of a comprehensive, integrated American early childhood system that makes high-quality early education available to all preschool age children on a voluntary basis.
- Establish *research-driven standards* regarding the expectations for children, the skills and competencies their teachers require, the provisions of programs that serve children, and the requirements for states regarding their duties in advancing the early childhood system." (pp. 47–48)

Goffin's call to action questions these two directives. Should a profession look to Washington to create vision and leadership for its work? Should Washington create the standards for children, teachers, and programs? In my experiences at both the state and federal levels, we used available policy levers to push specific programs and the larger ECE field forward—and at times we pushed very hard. We tried to lead the field from the policy arena—and given the absence of a shared set of ECE principles, I would repeat those actions. However, it may be time to change the all-too-familiar circumstances in which the ECE field waits for government leadership to define the basic elements of its own work: the body of knowledge, skills, and dispositions that are expected of young children and of early childhood professionals; expectations at each level of the professional career ladder that justify appropriate compensation; and elements of a monitoring and accountability system. Unless ECE owns these elements, the inevitable changing political perspectives can wreak havoc on the field's foundation.

Of course, state and federal policymakers still have an important role to play in increasing funding for program implementation and research and for facilitating greater coordination of state and federal programs. But government funding to improve ECE teacher and program quality and assessment and data systems should be *guided* by an agreed upon set of professional standards formed by the ECE profession.

It is time for a *field-driven* Council on ECE to convene and lay out a 3-year plan to professionalize the practice of early childhood education. Akin to Goffin's suggestion, a small group should convene to initiate honest reflection and critical exploration of questions such as those posed early in this discussion.

An ECE Council could embark on a listening tour to hear from practitioners, researchers, policymakers, and others. It could look to the history of other professions such as speech pathology and nursing and commission papers to guide ECE in the task of owning its work. If ECE, as a field of practice, defines itself, government can—as it should—play a strong supportive role rather than a profession-defining one. If not, the fault lies in ourselves.

## References

Barnett, W. S., Carolan, M. E., Fitzgerald, J., & Squires, J. H. (2011). *The state of preschool 2011: State preschool yearbook.* New Brunswick, NJ: National Institute for Early Education Research.

Kagan, S. L., & Reid, J. (2008). *Advancing ECE policy: Early childhood education (ECE) and its quest for excellence, coherence, and equity.* Washington, DC: Center on Education Policy.

---

MERGING TOWARD A UNIFIED FIELD OF PRACTICE

*Rolf Grafwallner*

---

In the spring of 2005, the Maryland General Assembly drafted a bill to transfer all child care functions to the state's department of education. Child care advocates, disappointed with the lack of support received from the state's social services agency, promoted the idea of consolidated governance in early childhood education (ECE), that is, to have all of the state's early care and education services overseen by the department of education. At the time, the proposal was controversial since it raised the thorny question of whether child care should be part of the education mandate and whether child care providers should be considered teachers.

## Forging a Single Discipline of Practice

While the governance of child care was resolved with the governor's signature, the underlying issue of two disciplines—child care and education—being merged into one, remains controversial. However, unified governance creates opportunities for improving the workforce credentials of those who are joining and those who have been part of the ECE field for many years.

From the onset, these two sectors of the ECE workforce have represented more differences than commonalities. In our state, 4-year-olds in public school Pre-Kindergarten are taught by teachers required to hold a state teaching certificate in ECE, while 4-year-olds in licensed child care centers can be taught by child care providers with 90 clock hours of training beyond a high school degree. The situation is not different in other states.

*ECE for a New Era* explains in detail the fallacies of such fragmentation and proposes as a solution a unified profession with a workforce defined by common expectations and clearer understanding of what we mean by a newly defined early childhood educator.

For states charged with reforming ECE systems, including the system of workforce development, the call for organizing ECE as a field of practice could not come at a more opportune time. Resolving the challenge, however, does not lie in some kind of regulatory reform, where the state simply ramps up requirements for child care providers in an effort to close the credentialing gap between public school Pre-Kindergarten and child care. Rather, it lies in a carefully designed scaffold for improving child care practitioners' credentials over time. Yet currently missing in ECE are mechanisms that can translate common understanding of what teachers' competencies should be into a workable system of early childhood educator preparation and practice.

## A Way Forward

The field currently has two major, albeit widely disparate, workforce systems that define preparation for teaching young children in child care and in public school settings. On the one hand, post-secondary programs can lead to 2- or 4-year degrees in ECE and, ultimately, state certification in teaching. On the other hand, state-run approved training programs support specific training requirements in addition to a high school diploma for child care practitioners.

Over the past two decades, child care credentialing systems have been a cornerstone of the state's career ladder, which is designed to serve as the connecting bridge between these two workforce sectors. Those in the child care workforce with an incomplete degree or no post-secondary education may access public funding to improve their credentials through continued training or additional college credits. However, what is still missing are two additional workforce development infrastructure components—alternative pathways to teacher licensure and on-the-job apprenticing (in today's jargon, residencies.)

At the upper end of a child care credentialing career ladder, early childhood teachers with 4-year degrees and who are working full-time face a steep, almost insurmountable obstacle when attempting to obtain state licensure as a teacher. In most states, licensure includes a stint in student teaching, passing the PRAXIS II exam, and completion of a teacher induction program, such as a full-term residency at a professional development school. The remedy could be an alternative preparation program leading to state licensure as exists in most states for career changers who are interested in transferring their skills from one discipline and applying it to teaching. What works for a chemist teaching chemistry should be applicable for a graduate in child development or psychology who is interested in teaching Kindergarten or Pre-Kindergarten. State policies that allow for alternative teacher preparation programs create pathways that lead to the professionalization of teaching (i.e., a state's licensure in teaching).

At the lower end of the child care credentialing career ladder, child care practitioners could benefit from a formal apprenticeship or residency that establishes expectations for both the operator of the child care program and the apprentice. As more training and on-the-job training sharpen skills and competence, child care credentialing systems could incorporate specified state child care certificates or credentials linked to regulatory reform and compensatory systems. For instance, to support evolution to state licensure, the current national Child Development Associate (CDA) credential could serve as the minimum qualification for caregivers. A newly devised CDA II could respond to a combination of training and residency requirements as well as a specified post-secondary degree such as an Associate of Arts Degree (AA) in Science or Teaching. The next level, a completed post-secondary four-year degree, could offer specialized post-B.A. certificates in inclusive care, cultural and linguistic diversity, or behavioral support.

Proposed enhancements at both the upper and lower ends of the child care credentialing system, in conjunction with a set of nationally recognized credentials and an alternative pathway to state licensure in teaching, could set the stage for a unified system of preparation and continuous education for child care and public school Pre-Kindergarten teachers. Its feasibility would be enhanced by building on the existing, currently distinct and separate, infrastructures of post-secondary teacher preparation, child care career ladders, and approved child care training systems. However, such a progressive system would have to be accompanied with regulatory reform, that is, licensing regulations, and a compensatory system, that is, compensation schedules, in order to create clear expectations and incentives for members of the workforce.

K–12 is currently undergoing complex and painful changes to create a newly minted workforce for a globally competitive education system. There should be room for ECE to prepare itself for a similar process of systems change by creating a unified workforce so confusion of what to call the classroom professional and what we can expect of them is a relic of the past.

## LEAPFROGGING COMPLEXITIES OF THE STATUS QUO

*Pamela J. Winton*

*Early Childhood Education for a New Era* is a catalyst for moving forward to solve a central problem plaguing our field: variability of early childhood education (ECE) program quality within and across communities. The primary reason for this challenge, according to Goffin, is the fact that ECE is not a defined profession with a well-articulated scope of practice coupled with competent and accountable practitioners. Not only that, it lacks the fieldwide leadership to become one, thereby abdicating responsibility and letting others, notably policymakers, define us as a field of practice.

This is a provocative charge, likely to provoke defensiveness, especially on the part of leaders. In my view, Goffin makes a convincing case, grounded in logic and literature, and I'm ready to jump on board. I especially resonate with Goffin's suggestion to address the field's fragmentation by considering "ECE as a profession of subfields," each recognized for its unique contributions, yet "bound together by a common overarching purpose, expert body of knowledge, and shared professional identity." To develop this idea, Goffin suggests bringing together a "microcosm of the field" to explore how to integrate "the parts to create a new whole," noting that reaching consensus and building leadership are essential to this process.

Like "motherhood and apple pie" most people embrace the concepts that fragmentation is problematic, consensus is needed, and cross-sector leadership and support are required. Yet, based on experiences working with colleagues supporting states in moving toward an integrated cross-sector early childhood professional development system (National Professional Development Center on Inclusion, 2011; Winton & Catlett,

2009; Winton, McCollum & Catlett, 2008), I have learned that the devil lies in the details. This reality focuses my "conversation starter," which I've organized around three devilish questions.

## Which Subfields Would Comprise the ECE Profession?

Goffin identifies a number of specialty groups (e.g., Head Start, family child care, early interventionists/early childhood special educators [EI/ECSE]), for possible inclusion as subfields comprising the ECE profession. Careful consideration as to how this would play out is warranted, though, especially given that some specialty subfields (e.g., EI/ECSE) are tightly intertwined with allied health disciplines (e.g., occupational therapy, speech and hearing sciences, special education). Defining the boundaries and relationships between and among subfields and their related non-ECE disciplines will be an important next task.

## What Entities or Individuals Represent Each Subfield?

Professional organizations, as the voice of their members, are an obvious choice for involvement. Goffin notes that because of their focus on serving their discrete membership, professional organizations are not necessarily logical leaders of ECE cross-sector/whole field change initiatives. Multiple financial, administrative, and structural concerns and questions are likely to surface. What should be the relationship among these organizations? Should the existing ECE membership organizations merge into a larger umbrella organization with subdivisions? Should a group of professional organizations form a leadership coalition as part of the profession's leadership infrastructure?

The call for adaptive and transformational leaders who can mobilize individuals to deal with change is a ubiquitous theme in *ECE for a New Era*. Taking the thinking a step further, what is the nature of adaptive and transformational leadership when it involves integrating existing sectors to create a new field? I suspect that breaking through the status quo will necessitate "edge" individuals, a term adopted from biology (Smith, 1974, p. 251) to define highly adaptable species able to exist successfully in the boundaries between ecosystems. In the case of ECE this refers to individuals capable of existing between subfields (e.g., Head Start, Pre-K, child care, EI/ECSE). Although these "edge" individuals might not typically be recognized as national leaders, they may be key to breaking down sector barriers at state and local levels.

## What Are Tasks Associated with Next Steps?

Fixsen and colleagues at the National Implementation Research Network (NIRN) talk about the importance of assessing "readiness for change" when moving forward in a complicated change initiative (Fixsen et al., 2009). Their framework for assessing readiness has application for the work of the proposed "microcosm" group. Readiness tasks include agreeing upon the *need* for ECE to organize as a profession, examining how the concept *fits* with existing initiatives, identifying the *resources and supports* needed for implementation, agreeing upon *outcomes* that would result if an ECE profession emerged, and building *readiness and capacity* for the field to implement and sustain the profession's goals.

Goffin articulates a *need* for ECE to become a profession; will others buy it? In terms of *fit*, Goffin asserts that working within the field's existing paradigm is part of the problem; her challenge to the field is to leapfrog the status quo. Perhaps it is a question of balance between making incremental changes within a broader paradigm shift propelled by actions of the "microcosm" group. The initial *resources and supports* needed for exploration by a small group might be supported by a philanthropic organization. Identifying the resources to finance all the phases involved in becoming and sustaining a new profession, however, may at first appear daunting. Yet when compared to the price of maintaining inefficiencies and duplications of the status quo, the costs may emerge as less overwhelming, especially if results for children are improved–but this assumption would need to be tested. The attributes of recognized professions (e.g., clarity of purpose, scope of practice, common knowledge) identified by Goffin provide the *outcome* focus for the effort as well as structure for *implementation and sustainability*. This brief assessment highlights leadership, resources, and commitment as the field's largest transformational challenges.

Goffin asserts that the choice is ours: staying stuck, while tinkering around the edges of addressing big challenges within our safe silos or, alternatively, choosing to change. No doubt, starting with a microcosm group that grows with the planning process could lead to macro-level and perhaps transformative change. Still I worry about being defeated by the devil in the details and moving beyond lip service to the concepts associated with cross-sector collaboration. Clearly, leaping forward will require time, patience, and courage from us all.

# References

Fixsen, D. L., Blase, K. A., Horner, R., & Sugai, G. (2009). Readiness for change. Scaling Up Brief #3. Available at http://sisep.fpg.unc.edu/sites/sisep.fpg.unc.edu/files/resources

National Professional Development Center on Inclusion (NPDCI). (2011). *The big picture: Building cross-sector professional development systems in early childhood* (3rd ed.). Available at http://npdci.fpg.unc.edu/sites/npdci.fpg.unc.edu/files/resources

Smith, R. L. (1974). *Ecology and field biology* (2nd ed.). New York: Harper & Row.

Winton, P., & Catlett, C. (2009). Statewide efforts to enhance early childhood personnel preparation programs to support inclusion: Overview and lessons learned. *Infants & Young Children, 22,* 63–70.

Winton, P., McCollum, J. A., & Catlett, C. (2008). A framework and recommendations for a cross-agency professional development system. In P. Winton, J. A. McCollum, & C. Catlett (Eds.), *Practical approaches to early childhood professional development: Evidence, strategies, and resources* (pp. 263–272). Washington, DC: Zero to Three.

# APPENDIX

# It's Time to Call the Question

"Until the nursery school and the nursery educators can clarify their roles and functions, they cannot effectively give to parents the reassurances and support needed in the family for acceptance and collaborating with the school in the shared responsibilities of early childhood education." (Lawrence K. Frank, Address given at NANE's[1] Biennial Conference, 1951, p. 6)

"With the withdrawal of federal funds at the end of the war and the consequent cessation of a national program of nursery schools, this level of our profession is left with a mixed heritage, a varied tradition. Neither National program, the depression nurseries nor the war nurseries, were set up to demonstrate educational values for children; rather, they were to facilitate employment of adults. Is that our status as a profession? Are we adjuncts to research centers as in the beginning period of our history? Are we, or should we be, social service agencies providing a coordinating center for community interests, a private school luxury, or a beginning class in public schools?" (Winifred E. Bain, 1955, p. 9)

"There is no substitute for this specialized profession and although semantically it may be variously titled in different academic and geographical settings . . . . herein rests a body of knowledge and experience that is unique and of vital importance to all other professions concerned with human behaviors. It will be proposed in this paper, that the preschool educators accept the responsibility for working towards the maturation of its profession." (Judith A. Schoenlkopf, Address presented at NANE's Biennial Conference, 1957, p. 9)

"How nursery school teachers should be prepared for their professional work has been a confused matter of discussion, writing and sporadic action for years. . . . Are we, the professional nursery school teachers, getting anywhere with our discussions and writing? Are we coming closer to commonly-agreed-upon goals and plans of action? Or are we being

pushed hither and yon by 'reality'–the reality of public opinion, the num-
bers of young children being placed in group programs, the low salaries
paid teachers, licensing laws, the variety and divisiveness among ourselves?" . . . "Will the profession guide its own destiny or will it allow
itself to be shaped by the other three definers of standards-government
licensing agencies, preparing institutions, hiring institutions?" (Evange-
line Burgess, 1961, pp. 9, 13)

"It has been said–and rightly–that our differences appear greater than
our commonality. It has been said–and rightly–that we are breaking into
such small sub-groups that we may be forcing ourselves out of existence."
(Glenn Hawkes, president, NANE, 1962, p. 45)

"What is our [NAEYC] role? To clarify the confusion in semantics–day
care, day nursery, kindergarten, nursery school, early childhood, child
care center, preschool, and the like." (Cornelia Goldsmith, NAEYC's first
executive director, explaining the intent of the transition from NANE to
NAEYC, 1965, p. 212)

"While a great deal of attention is currently being given to fostering concept formation in young children, there appears to be relatively little concern with concept formation *about* the field most intimately concerned
with child development. Why can we not be more explicit about our
goals and objectives?" (Bettye Caldwell, 1967, p. 348)

"Within the field, we need to continue to try to increase our understanding of who and what we are and to feel more confident about our contributions to the welfare of children and families. We need to decide what
we want to be called and disseminate this terminology to the general public so that it becomes part of our everyday language." (Bettye Caldwell,
1983, p. 15)

"We *must* unify the field of early childhood education. The greatest obstacle, and yet the one that could have the most positive impact on services
to children and their families, is to find ways to negate the dichotomies
that split our field apart." (Marilyn Smith, 1987, p. 38)

"The early childhood educator role requires professional attitudes and behaviors, although early childhood education does not meet the standards
of a profession. With its shaky knowledge base, its ambiguous clientele,

and its lack of a code of ethics, early childhood education qualifies only as an occupation or, at best, a semiprofession." (Milly Almy, 1988, p. 50)

"The evolution of the early childhood field is that of several movements . . . That these movements continue to have a separateness and have yet to come together under one conceptualization of early childhood education is central to understanding the debate surrounding issues of professionalism." (Bernard Spodek, Olivia Saracho, & Donald Peters, 1988, p. 3)

"The profession must bear some of the responsibility for low quality. . . . We have forged little agreement regarding the kind or amount of training needed by direct service providers, much less by managers, trainers, allied professionals, or supervisors." (Barbara T. Bowman, 2001, p. 176)

"One major challenge, while also predictable, was of such transcendental importance that we wrestled with it daily. The lack of definitional clarity has characterized the field for decades, with numerous debates regarding what to call this important work: early education, early childhood education, early care and education, preschool. . . . Even more problematic, however, is the field's inconsistent use of terms . . . teachers, workforce, turnover, professional development, education, and training." (Sharon Lynn Kagan, Kristie Kauerz, & Kate Tarrant, 2008, pp. x–xi)

". . . .to define the scope and nature of professional development, the profession needs to be defined." (Sharon Lynn Kagan & Rebecca E. Gomez, 2011, p. 73)

# Notes

## Chapter 2

1. Barbara Bowman, personal communication, December 17, 2012.
2. This phrase is taken from *One strong voice: The story of the American Nurses Association.*

## Chapter 3

1. This word choice comes from Winifred Bain (1955), who, in comments on the state of nursery education as a profession, suggested it as a term offering more flexibility than *standardization*. Bain served as the second president of Wheelock College.
2. Morgan (1994b) created iterative versions of this document based on discussions at conferences. Most of these versions were not dated. This version to my understanding represents one of the last iterations.

## Chapter 4

1. Burchinal, Hyson, & Zaslow, 2011; Hyson, Horm, & Winton, 2012; Whitebook, Austin, Ryan, et al., 2012 examine variability in the organization of ECE teacher preparation.
2. Responding to the question of who should be recognized as part of the ECE field, the IOM and NRC (2012) defined the *occupation* as paid work involving direct care and education of children from birth through age 5. The *sector* includes the occupation as well as those working for establishments providing direct services to children, such as administrators and cooks. The *enterprise* includes the sector as well as those whose paid work has a direct effect on practice, such as licensing officials and teacher preparation faculty. Alternatively, NAEYC (n.d.) defines early childhood professionals as individuals providing direct services to young children from birth through age 8 and their families as well as

those administering programs in which these individuals work plus those providing professional development for them.

3. My appreciation to Sue Bredekamp for heightening my sensitivity to these realities.

4. This "new" interest isn't really new. It mirrors the field's focus on teacher-child interactions prior to the 1960s. New is its conceptualization as an intervention strategy.

5. Sullivan (2005a) uses slightly different language: intellectual sophistication, practical skills, and a strong sense of public responsibility.

6. Mitchell (1996) posed a similar possibility, even positing the possibility that not all occupations within the field would be deemed professional.

7. See Galinsky & Weissbourd, 1992; Zero to Three, n.d.; Zigler, 1999 for complementary views.

## Chapter 5

1. The notion of getting unstuck is taken from Kahane (2012).

2. A growing body of literature and experience informs change efforts such as these. For example: adaptive leadership (Heifetz, 1994; Heifetz, Grashow, & Linsky, 2009; Heifetz & Linsky, 2002); transformational leadership (Kahane, 2010, 2012; Senge et al., 2005, 2010); systems change (Senge, 1990; Senge et al., 1999, 2010); dialogue (Brown & Issacs, 2005; Issacs, 1999); mobilizing change (Heifetz, Grashow, & Linsky, 2009; Kotter, 1996, 2008; Kouzes & Posner, 1997).

3. The term "microcosm" in this context comes from Senge et al. (2010).

## Appendix

1. National Association for Nursery Education, the forerunner of the National Association for the Education of Young Children (NAEYC).

# References

*Please note that online sources may have changed since the original date the source was retrieved.*

Almy, A. (1988). The early childhood educator revisited. In B. Spodek, O. N. Saracho, & D. L. Peters (Eds.), *Professionalism and the early childhood practitioner* (pp. 48–55). New York: Teachers College Press.

American Nurses Association. (2004). *Nursing: Scope & standards of practice.* Washington, DC: Author.

American Nurses Association. (2010). *Recognition of a nursing specialty, approval of a specialty nursing scope of practice statement, and acknowledgement of specialty nursing standards of practice.* Silver Springs, MD: Author.

Antler, J. (1987). *Lucy Sprague Mitchell: The making of a modern woman.* New Haven, CT: Yale University Press.

Bain, W. E. (1955). The state of the profession. *NANE Bulletin, 11*(1), 7–11.

Barnett, W. S. (1993). New wine in old bottles: Increasing the coherence of early childhood care and education policy. *Early Childhood Research Quarterly, 8,* 519–558.

Barnett, W. S. (2011). Effectiveness of early educational intervention. *Science, 333,* 975–978.

Beatty, B. (1990). "A vocation from on high": Kindergartening as an occupation for American women. In J. Antler & S. K. Biklen (Eds.), *Changing education: Women as radicals and conservators* (pp. 35–50). Albany, NY: SUNY Press.

Bellm, D., & Whitebook, M. (2006). *Roots of decline: How government policy has de-educated teachers of young children.* Berkeley, CA: Center for the Study of Child Care Employment, Institute of Industrial Relations, University of California at Berkeley.

Benedict, R. (1948). What are we educating for? *Bulletin of the National Association for Nursery Education, III* (2), 5–9.

Biber, B. (Ed.). (1984). Images of school influence: Social change and child personality. In *Early education and psychological development* (pp. 8–14). New Haven, CT: Yale University Press.

Bogard, K., Traylor, F., & Takaishi, R. (2008). Teacher education and pre-k outcomes: Are we asking the right questions? *Early Childhood Research Quarterly, 23*(1), 1–6.

Bowman, B. T. (1981). Standards for professional practice, *Young Children, 37*(1), 56–57.

Bowman, B. (2001). Facing the future. In *NAEYC at 75. Reflections on the past. Challenges for the future* (pp. 167–182). Washington, DC: National Association for the Education of Young Children.

Bowman, B. T. (2007, November). *How I got hooked on learning standards.* Presentation at the annual meeting of the National Association of Early Childhood Specialists in State Departments of Education, Chicago, IL.

Bowman, B. T. (2011). Bachelor's degrees are necessary but not sufficient. In E. Zigler, W. S. Gilliam, & W. S. Barnett (Eds.), *The pre-k debates: Current controversies & issues* (pp. 54–57). Baltimore: Paul H. Brookes.

Bowman, B. T., Donovan, M. S., & Burns, M. S. (Eds.). (2001). *Eager to learn: Educating our preschoolers.* National Research Council, Committee on Early Childhood Pedagogy. Commission on Behavioral and Social Sciences and Education. Washington, DC: National Academy Press.

Bowman, B. T., & Kagan, S. L. (Eds.). (1997). Moving the leadership agenda. In *Leadership in early care and education* (pp. 157–160). Washington, DC: National Association for the Education of Young Children.

Brandon, E. D., Jr., & Welch, H. O. (2009). *The history of financial planning: The transformation of financial services.* Hoboken, NJ: Wiley.

Bredekamp, S. (Ed.). (1986). *Developmentally appropriate practice.* Washington, DC: National Association for the Education of Young Children.

Bredekamp, S. (1992a). Composing a profession, *Young Children, 47*(2), 52–54.

Bredekamp, S. (1992b). The early childhood profession coming together. *Young Children, 47*(6), 36–39.

Bredekamp, S. (2004, June). *Critical issues in early childhood education workforce development.* Paper prepared for the Cantingy Conference on The Field of Early Childhood Education Professional Development: Implications for Teaching, Research, and Policy, Chicago, IL.

Bredekamp, S. (2011). *Effective practices in early childhood education.* Upper Saddle River, NJ: Pearson.

Bredekamp, S., & Goffin, S. G. (2012). Making the case: Why credentialing and certification matter. In R. C. Pianta, S. W. Barnett, L. M. Justice, & S. M. Sheridan (Eds.), *Handbook of early childhood education* (pp. 584–604). New York: Guilford Press.

Bredekamp, S., & Willer, B. (1992). Of ladders and lattices, cores and cones: Conceptualizing an early childhood professional development system. *Young Children, 47*(3), 47–50.

Bredekamp, S., & Willer, B. (1993). Professionalizing the field of early childhood education: Pros and cons. *Young Children, 48*(3), 82–84.

Brown, J., & Issacs, D. (2005). *The world café: Shaping our futures through conversations that matter.* San Francisco: Berrett-Koehler.

Bruner, C. (2004). *Beyond the usual suspects: Developing new allies to invest in school readiness.* Des Moines, IA: State Early Childhood Policy Technical Assistance Network.

Bueno, M., Darling-Hammond, L., & Gonzales, D. (2010). A matter of degrees: Preparing teachers for the pre-k classroom. *The Pew Center on the States, Education Reform Series.* Washington, DC: The Pew Charitable Trusts.

Burchinal, M., Hyson, M., & Zaslow, M. (2011). Competencies and credentials for early childhood educators. In E. Zigler, W. S. Gilliam, & W. S. Barnett (Eds.), *The pre-k debates: Current controversies & issues* (pp. 73–76). Baltimore: Paul H. Brookes.

Burgess, E. (1961). Standards for teacher education–A challenge to NANE. *The Journal of Nursery Education, 17*(1), 9–14

Burns, J. M. (2010). *Leadership.* New York: Harper Perennial Political Classics. (Original work published 1978)

Cahan, E. (1989). *Past caring: A history of U.S. preschool care and education for the poor, 1820–1965.* New York: National Center for Children in Poverty.

Caldwell, B. M. (1967). On reformulating the concept of early childhood education: Some whys needing wherefores. *Young Children, 22*(6), 348–356.

Caldwell, B. M. (1983). How can we educate the American public about the child care profession? *Young Children, 38*(3), 11–17.

Camfield, T. M. (1973). The professionalization of American psychology, 1870–1917. *Journal of the History of the Behavioral Sciences, 9*(1), 66–75.

The Carnegie Foundation for the Advancement of Teaching. (June 29, 2010). Educating nurses and physicians: Toward new horizons. A Webinar. Accompanying slides available at http://www.carnegiefoundation.org/sites/default/files/assets/CFAT-MACY_webinar.pdf

Center for the Advancement of Social Entrepreneurship. (2008). Developing the field of social entrepreneurship: A report from the Center for the Advancement of Social Enterpreneurship (CASE). Center for the Advancement of Social Entrepreneurship Duke University: The Fuqua School of Business. Available at http://www.caseatduke.org/documents/CASE_Field-Building_Report_June08.pdf

The Children's Partnership. (1996, July). Building a constituency for children: Community and national strategies. Wingspread Conference summary and highlights. Washington, DC: Author.

Clarke-Stewart, K. A. (1988). Evolving issues in early childhood education: A personal perspective. *Early Childhood Research Quarterly, 3*, 139–149.

Coalition for America's Children with the Benton Foundation. (1999, May). *Effective language for communicating children's issues.* Washington, DC: Coalition for America's Children.

Cohen, S. S. (2001). *Championing child care.* New York: Columbia University Press.

Copple, C., & Bredekamp, S. (Eds.). (2009). *Developmentally appropriate practice in early childhood programs,* third edition. Washington, DC: National Association for the Education of Young Children.

Cravens, H. (1985). Child-saving in the age of professionalism, 1915–1930. In J. M. Hawes & N. R. Hiner (Eds.), *American childhood: A research guide and historical handbook* (pp. 415–488). Westport, CT: Greenwood Press.

Cravens, H. (1993). *Before Head Start: The Iowa Station and America's children.* Chapel Hill, NC: The University of North Carolina Press.

Dower, C., O'Neil, E., & Hough, H. J. (2001, September). *Profiling the professions: A model for evaluating emerging health professions.* San Francisco, CA: Center for the Health Professions, University of California, San Francisco. Available at http://www.soundrock.com/sop/pdf/Profiling%20the%20Professions.pdf

Dreeben, R. (2005). Teaching and the competence of organizations. In L. V. Hedges & B. Schneider (Eds.), *The social organization of schooling* (pp. 51–71). New York: Russell Sage Foundation.

Drucker, P. F. (2003). *The new realities.* New Brunswick, NJ: Transaction. (Original work published 1989)

Early, D., Barbarin, O., Bryant, D., Burchinal, M., Chang, F., Clifford, R., . . . Weaver, W. (2005, May). *Pre-kindergarten in eleven states: NCEDL's multi-state study of pre-kindergarten & study of state-wide early education programs (SWEEP). Preliminary descriptive report.* Available at http://www.fpg.unc.edu/resources/kindergarten-eleven-states-ncedls-multistate-study-pre-kindergarten-study-state-wide

Early, D. M., Bryant, D. M., Pianta, R. C., Clifford, R. M., Burchinal, M. R., Ritchie, S., & Barbarin, O. (2006). Are teachers' education, major, and credential related to classroom quality and children's academic gains in pre-kindergarten? *Early Childhood Research Quarterly, 21,* 174–195.

Elhauge, E. R. (May 31, 2006). *Can health law become a coherent field of law?* Available at http://lawreview.law.wfu.edu/documents/issue.41.365.pdf

Feeney, S. (2012). *Professionalism in early childhood education: Doing our best for children.* Upper Saddle River, NJ: Pearson.

Finkelstein, B. (1988). The revolt against selfishness: Women and the dilemmas of professionalism in early childhood education. In B. Spodek, O. N. Saracho, & D. L. Peters (Eds.), *Professionalism and the early childhood practitioner* (pp. 10–28). New York: Teachers College Press.

Flanagan, L. (1976). *One strong voice: The story of the American Nurses Association.* Kansas City, MO: The American Nurses Association.

Frank, L. K. (1951). These years–Children's opportunities and responsibilities. *NANE Bulletin, VI* (3), 3–10.

Freeman, K., & Feeney, S. (2006). The new face of early care and education: Who are we? Where are we going? *Young Children, 61*(5), 10–16.

Freidson, E. (2001). *Professionalism: The third logic.* Chicago: The University of Chicago Press.

Fullan, M. (1998). Leadership for the 21st century: Breaking the bonds of dependency. *Educational Leadership, 55*(1), 6–10.

Fullan, M. (April 2011, April). *Choosing the wrong drivers for whole system reform,* (Seminar Series Paper No. 204). East Melbourne, Australia: Centre for Strategic Education.

Fullan, M., & Hargreaves, A. (June 6, 2012). Reviving teaching with "professional capital." *Education Week, 31*(33), 36, 30.

Fuller, B. (2007). *Standardized childhood: The political and cultural struggle over early education.* Stanford, CA: Stanford University Press.

Fuller, B., & Holloway, S. D. (1996). When the state innovates: Interests and institutions create the preschool sector. In A. Pallas (Ed.), *Research in sociology of education* (Vol. 2, pp. 1–42). Oxford, UK: Elsevier.

Galinsky, E., & Weissbourd, B. (1992). Family-centered child care. In B. Spodek & O. N. Saracho (Eds.), *Issues in child care* (pp. 47–65). New York: Teachers College Press.

Gardner, H., & Schulman, L. S. (Summer 2005). The professions in America today: Crucial but fragile. *Daedalus, 134*(3), 13–18.

Garwood, S. G., Phillips, D., Hartman, A., & Zigler, E. F. (1989). As the pendulum swings: Federal agency programs for children. *American Psychologist, 44*(2), 434–440.

Goffin, S. G. (2001). Whither early childhood care and education in the new century? In L. Corno (Ed.), *Education across a century: The centennial volume.* One hundredth yearbook of the National Society for the Study of Education, Part I (pp. 140–163). Chicago: National Society for the Study of Education.

Goffin, S. G. (2009). *Field-wide leadership: Insights from five fields of practice.* Washington, DC: The Goffin Strategy Group. Available at www.goffinstrategygroup.com

Goffin, S. G. (2012). Beyond systemic structures: Penetrating to the core of an early care and education system. In S. L. Kagan & K. Kauerz (Eds.), *Early childhood systems: Transforming early learning* (pp. 267–282). New York: Teachers College Press.

Goffin, S. G., & Janke, M. (2013, May). *Early childhood education leadership development compendium: A view of the current landscape* (2nd ed.). Washington, DC: Goffin Strategy Group. Available at www.goffinstrategygroup.com

Goffin, S. G., & Means, K. M. (2009, September). *Leadership development in early care and education: A view of the current landscape.* Washington, DC: Goffin Strategy Group. Available at www.goffinstrategygroup.com

Goffin, S. G., & Washington, V. (2007). *Ready or not: Leadership choices in early care and education.* New York: Teachers College Press.

Goffin, S. G., & Wilson, C. S. (2001). *Curriculum models and early childhood education: Appraising the relationship* (2nd ed.). Upper Saddle River, NJ: Merrill Prentice Hall.

Goldsmith, C. (1965). The impact of a growing NAEYC on young children. *Young Children, 20*(4), 209–212.

Goodlad, J. I. (1990). The occupation of teaching in schools. In J. I. Goodlad, R. Soder, & K. A. Sirotnik (Eds.), *The moral dimensions of teaching* (pp. 3–34). San Francisco, CA: Jossey-Bass.

Greenberg, P. (1969). *The devil has slippery shoes: A biased biography of the child development group of Mississippi (CDGM), a story of maximum feasible poor parent participation.* London, UK: The Macmillan Company, Collier-Macmillan Limited.

Grubb, W. N., & Lazerson, M. (1982, 1988). *Broken promises: How Americans fail their children.* Chicago: The University of Chicago Press.

Haberman, M. (1988). Gatekeepers to the profession. In B. Spodek, O. N. Saracho, & D. L. Peters (Eds.), *Professionalism and the early childhood practitioner* (pp. 84–92). New York: Teachers College Press.

Hawkes, G. (1962). Why join the National Association for Nursery Education? *The Journal of Nursery Education, 17*(2), 45.

Heifetz, R. A. (1994). *Leadership without easy answers.* Cambridge, MA: Belknap Press of Harvard University Press.

Heifetz, R., Grashow, A., & Linsky, M. (2009). *The practice of adaptive leadership: Tools and tactics for changing your organization and the world.* Boston: Harvard Business Press.

Heifetz, R. A., & Linsky, M. (2002). *Leadership on the line: Staying alive through the dangers of leading.* Boston: Harvard Business School Press.

Herasymowych, M., & Senko, H. (June/July 2012). "Positive" system archetypes. *The Systems Thinker, 15*(5), 6–8.

Hess, R. D., Price, G. G., Dickson, W. P., & Conroy, M. (1981). Different roles for mothers and teachers: Contrasting styles of child care. In S. Kilmer (Ed.), *Advances in early education and day care* (Vol. 2, pp. 1–28). Greenwich, CT: JAI Press.

Hewes, D., and the NAEYC Organizational History and Archives Committee. (2001). In *NAEYC at 75. Reflections on the past. Challenges for the future* (pp. 35–52). Washington, DC: National Association for the Education of Young Children.

Huston, A. (2012). In IOM (Institute of Medicine) and NRC (National Research Council), *The early childhood care and education workforce: Challenges and opportunities: A workshop report* (pp. ix–xi). Washington, DC: The National Academies Press.

Hyson, M., Horm, D. M., & Winston, P. J. (2012). Higher education for early childhood educators and outcomes for young children: Pathways toward greater effectiveness. In R. C. Pianta, S. W. Barnett, L. M. Justice, & S. M. Sheridan (Eds.), *Handbook of early childhood education* (pp. 553–583). New York: Guilford Press.

IOM (Institute of Medicine) and NRC (National Research Council). (2012). *The early childhood care and education workforce: Challenges and opportunities: A workshop report.* Washington, DC: The National Academies Press.

Issacs, D. (1999). *Dialogue and the art of thinking together.* New York: Currency.

Iyengar, S. (2010). *The art of choosing.* New York: Twelve.

Kagan, S. L. (2012). Early learning and development standards: An elixir for early childhood systems reform. In S. L. Kagan & K. Kauerz (Eds.), *Early childhood systems: Transforming early learning* (pp. 55–70). New York: Teachers College Press.

Kagan, S. L., & Cohen, N. E. (1997). *Not by chance: Creating an early care and education system for America's children.* Full Report, The Quality 2000 Initiative. New Haven, CT: The Bush Center for Child Development and Social Policy.

Kagan, S. L., & Gomez, R. E. (2011). B.A. plus: Reconciling reality and reach, In E. Zigler, W. S. Gilliam, & W. S. Barnett (Eds.), *The pre-k debates: Current controversies & issues* (pp. 68–73). Baltimore: Paul H. Brookes.

Kagan, S. L., & Kauerz, K. (2007). Reaching for the whole: Integration and alignment in early education policies. In R. C. Pianta, M. J. Cox, & K. L. Snow (Eds.), *School readiness and the transition to kindergarten in the era of accountability* (pp. 3–30). Baltimore: Paul H. Brookes.

Kagan, S. L., & Kauerz, K. (2012). Early childhood systems: Looking deep, wide, and far. In S. L. Kagan & K. Kauerz (Eds.), *Early childhood systems: Transforming early learning* (pp. 3–17). New York: Teachers College Press.

Kagan, S. L., Kauerz, K., & Tarrant, K. (2008). *The early care and education teaching workforce at the fulcrum.* New York: Teachers College Press.

Kahane, A. (2010). *Power and love: A theory and practice of social change.* San Francisco: Berrett-Koehler.

Kahane, A. (2012). *Working together to change the future: Transformative scenario planning.* San Francisco: Berrett-Koehler.

Katz, L. G. (Ed.). (1980). Mothering and teaching—Some significant distinctions. In *Current topics in early childhood education* (Vol. 3, pp. 47–63). Norwood, NJ: Ablex Publishing Corporation.

Katz, L. G. (1984). The professional preschool teacher. In L. G. Katz (Ed.), *More talks with teachers* (pp. 27–44). Urbana, IL: Clearinghouse on Elementary and Early Childhood Education, College of Education, University of Illinois.

Katz, L. G. (1988). Where is early childhood education as a profession? In B. Spodek, O. N. Saracho, & D. L. Peters (Eds.), *Professionalism and the early childhood practitioner* (pp. 75–83). New York: Teachers College Press.

Katz, L. G. (2007, November). Reflections on our field. Presentation delivered at the Annual Meeting of the National Association of Early Childhood Specialists–State Departments of Education, Chicago, IL.

Kegan, R., & Lahey, L. L. (2001). *How the way we talk can change the way we work: Seven languages for transformation.* San Francisco: Jossey-Bass.

Khurana, R., & Nohria, N. (2008). It's time to make management a true profession. *Harvard Business Review, 86*(10), 70–77.

Klein, A. G. (1992). *The debate over child care 1969-1990: A sociohistorical analysis.* Albany, NY: State University of New York Press.

Kotter, J. P. (1996). *Leading change.* Boston: Harvard Business Press.

Kotter, J. P. (2008). *A sense of urgency.* Boston: Harvard Business Press.

Kouzes, J. M., & Posner, B. Z. (1997). *The leadership challenge: How to keep getting extraordinary things done in organizations.* San Francisco: Jossey-Bass.

Kurtzman, J. (2010). *Common purpose: How great leaders get organizations to achieve the extraordinary.* San Francisco: Jossey-Bass.

Landry, S. H., Swank, P. R., Smith, K. E., Assel, M. A., & Gunnewigh, S. B. (2006). Enhancing early literacy skills for preschool children: Bringing a professional development model to scale. *Journal of Learning Disabilities, 39*, 306–324.

Lazerson, M. (1971). Social reform and early childhood education: Some historical perspectives. In R. H. Anderson & H. G. Shane (Eds.), *As the twig is bent* (pp. 22-33). Boston: Houghton Mifflin.

Lazerson, M. (1972). The historical antecedents of early childhood education: Some historical perspectives. In I. J. Gordon & H. G. Richey (Eds.), *Early childhood education.* Seventy-first Yearbook of the National Society for the Study of Education, Part 2 (pp. 33–53). Chicago: National Society for the Study of Education.

LeMoine, S. (2008). *Workforce designs: A policy blueprint for state early childhood professional development systems.* Washington, DC: National Association for the Education of Young Children.

Linsky, M., & Heifetz, R. (2007). Foreword. In S. G. Goffin & V. Washington (Eds.), *Ready or not: Leadership choices in early care and education* (pp. ix–xi). New York: Teachers College Press.

Lortie, D. C. (1969). The balance of control and autonomy in elementary school. In A. Etzioni (Ed.), *The semi-professions and their organization* (pp. 1–53). New York: The Free Press.

Maxwell, K. L., Lim, C. I., & Early, D. M. (2006). *Early childhood teacher preparation programs in the United States: National report.* Chapel Hill, NC: FPG Child Development Institute, University of North Carolina.

Mead, S., & Carey, K. (2011). *Beyond Bachelor's: The case for charter colleges of early childhood education.* Washington, DC: The Brookings-Rockefeller Project on State and Metropolitan Innovation.

Merton, R. K. (1958). The functions of the professional association. *The American Journal of Nursing, 58*(1), 50–54.

Metzger, W. P. (1987). A spectre is haunting American scholars: The spectre of "professionism." *Educational Researcher, 16*(6), 10–18.

Mitchell, A. (1996). Licensing: Lessons from other occupations. In S. L. Kagan & N. E. Cohen (Eds.), *Reinventing early care and education: A vision for a quality system* (pp. 101–123). San Francisco: Jossey Bass.

Mitchell, A. (2012, August). Considerations for an efficient, inclusive and implementable Quality Rating and Improvement System. BUILD Initiative, QRIS National Learning Network. Available at http://qrisnetwork.org/sites/all/files/resources/gscobb/2012-08-03%2016:42/Considerations%20 for%20QRIS%20Standards.pdf

Mitchell, A., & Shore, R. (1999). *Next steps toward quality in early care and education.* A report commissioned by the Early Childhood Funders Collaborative.

Modigliani, K. (1993). *Child care as an occupation in a culture of indifference.* Boston: Wheelock College.

Morgan, G. G. (1994a). A new century/A new system for professional development. In J. Johnson & J. B. McCracken (Eds.), *The early childhood career lattice: Perspectives on professional development* (pp. 39–46). Washington, DC: National Association for the Education of Young Children.

Morgan, G. G. (1994b, November). *Is "professional" a noun?* Presented at the meeting of The Center for Career Development in Early Care and Education, Boston, MA.

Morgan, G. G., Azer, S. L., Costley, J. B., Genser, A., Goodman, I. F., Lombardi, J., & McGimsey, B. (1993). *Making a career of it: The state of the states report on career development in early care and education.* Boston: The Center for Career Development in Early Care and Education at Wheelock College.

Morgan, K. J. (2001). A child of the sixties: The Great Society, the New Right, and the politics of federal child care. *Journal of Policy History, 13*(2), 215–250.

Morgan, K. J. (Summer 2005). The "production" of child care: How labor markets shape social policy and vice versa. *Social Politics: International Studies in Gender, State, and Society, 12*(2), 243–263.

Naisbett, J. (2006). *Mind set!* New York: HarperCollins.

National Association for the Education of Young Children. (n.d.). *Who are early childhood professionals?* Available at http://www.naeyc.org/ecp/overview0/ecps

National Association for the Education of Young Children. (1994). Conceptual framework for the early childhood profession. Position statement. *Young Children, 48*(3), 69–76.

National Association for the Education of Young Children. (2001). *NAEYC at 75: Reflections on the past. Challenges for the future.* Washington, DC: Author.

National Association for the Education of Young Children. (2011). Code of ethical conduct and statement of commitment. Washington, DC: Author. Available at www.naeyc.org/files/naeyc/file/positions/Ethics%20Position%20 Statement2011.pdf

National Committee on Nursery Schools. (1929). *Minimum essentials for nursery education.* [Pamphlet]. Author.

National Governor's Association. (1990). *Educating America: State strategies for achieving the national education goals.* Washington, DC: Author.

National Institute for Early Childhood Professional Development. (1993). *Concept papers & National Institute for Professional Development background materials.* Washington, DC: National Association for the Education of Young Children.

Neugebauer, R. (1995). The movers and shapers of early childhood education. *Child Care Information Exchange,* 106, pp. 9–12.

Neugebauer, R. (2008). The name for our profession is . . . . *Exchange, 87*(180), 89.

Neugebauer, R. (2011). Qualifications of preschool teachers: A hot issue in our field. *Exchange, 33*(6), 23–28.

Office of Planning, Research, and Evaluation (OPRE). (2010). *Compendium of quality rating systems and evaluation.* Available at http://www.acf.hhs.gov/ programs/opre/cc/childcare_quality/

Pew Center on the States. (2011). *Mobilizing business champions for children: A guide for advocates.* Washington, DC: Author.

Pfeffer, J. (2011). Management as a profession: Where's the proof? *Harvard Business Review, 89*(9), 38.

Pianta, R. C. (2011). A degree is not enough: Teachers need stronger and more individualized professional development supports to be effective in the classroom. In E. Zigler, W. S. Gilliam, & W. S. Barnett (Eds.), *The pre-k debates: Current controversies & issues* (pp. 64–68). Baltimore: Paul H. Brookes.

Pianta, R. C. (2012). Taking seriously the needs and capacity of the early childhood care and education workforce. *Social Policy Report, 26*(1), 27–28.

Pianta, R. C., Barnett, W. S., Burchinal, M., & Thornburg, K. R. (2009). The effects of preschool education: What we know, how public policy is or is not aligned with the evidence base, and what we need to know. *Psychological Science in the Public Interest, 10*(2), 49–88.

Phillips, D., & Lowenstein, A. E. (2011). Early care, education, and development. *Annual Review of Psychology, 62*(1), 483–500.

Prahalad, C. K. (2010). The responsible manager. *Harvard Business Review. 88*(1), 36.

Race to the Top–Early Learning Challenge. (2011). Race to the Top–Early Learning Challenge (RTT-ELC) Program, U.S. Department of Education. Available at http://www.ed.gov/early-learning/elc-draft-summary

Ready, D. A., & Truelove, E. (2011). The power of collective ambition. *Harvard Business Review, 89*(2), 94–102.

Rhodes, H., & Huston, A. (2012). Building the workforce our youngest children deserve. *Social Policy Report, 26*(1), 3–26.

Rose, E. (2010). *The promise of preschool.* Oxford, UK: Oxford University Press.

Schoenlkopf, J. A. (1957). New directions for preschool education. *The Journal of Nursery Education, XIII*(1), 8–17.

Schulman, L. S. (2005). Signature pedagogies in the professions. *Daedalus,* 52–59.

Scott-Little, C., Kagan, S. L., & Frelow, V. S. (2006). Conceptualization of readiness and the content of early learning standards: The intersection of policy and research. *Early Childhood Research Quarterly, 21,* 153–173.

Senge, P. M. (1990). *The fifth discipline: The art and practice of the learning organization.* New York: Doubleday.

Senge, P., Kleiner, A., Robert, C., Ross, R., Roth, G., & Smith, B. (1999). *The dance of change: The challenge to sustaining momentum in learning organizations.*New York: Doubleday.

Senge, P., Scharmer, C. O., Jaworski, J., & Flowers, B. S. (2005). *Presence: An exploration of profound change in people, organizations, and society.* New York: Doubleday.

Senge, P., Smith, B., Kruschwitz, N., Laur, J., & Schley, S. (2010). *The necessary revolution: Working together to create a sustainable world.* New York: Broadway Books.

Shonkoff, J. P. (2010, October). *Creating the future of early childhood policy and practice.* Presentation at the From Neurons to Neighborhoods Anniversary: Ten Years Later. Institute of Medicine, National Research Council, Washington, DC.

Shonkoff, J. P. (2011). Protecting brains, not simply stimulating minds. *Science, 333,* 982–983.

Smith, M. (1987). NAEYC at 60: Visions for the year 2000. *Young Children, 42*(3), 33–39.

Smith, M. (1989). NAEYC: Confronting tough issues. *Young Children, 45*(1), 32–37.

Snyder, A. (1972). *Dauntless women in childhood education: 1856–1931.* Washington, DC: Association for Childhood Education International.

Spodek, B., Saracho, O. N., & Peters, D. L. (1988). Professionalism, semiprofessionalism, and craftsmanship. In B. Spodek, O. N. Saracho, & D. L. Peters (Eds.), *Professionalism and the early childhood practitioner* (pp. 3–9). New York: Teachers College Press.

Stendler, C. B. (1952). What is the responsibility of the nursery school teacher toward children? *NANE Bulletin, 7*(2), 13–16

Stone, C., & Travis, J. (2011, March). *Toward a new professionalism in policing.* Harvard Kennedy School National Institute of Justice. Available at http://www.ncjrs.gov/pdffiles1/nij/232359.pdf

Stookey, C. W. (2003). *The container principle: Resilience, chaos, and trust.* Halifax, Canada: The Nova Scotia Sea School.

Sullivan, W. M. (2005a). Markets vs. professions: Value added? *Daedalus, 134*(3), 19–26.

Sullivan, W. M. (2005b). *Work and integrity: The crisis and promise of professionalism in America* (2nd ed.). San Francisco: Jossey-Bass.

Sullivan, W. M. (2010, June). Educating nurses and physicians: Toward new horizons. The Carnegie Foundation for the Advancement of Teaching. [Webinar.] Accompanying slides available at http://www.carnegiefoundation.org/sites/default/files/assets/CFAT-MACY_webinar.pdf

Sykes, G. (1987). Reckoning with the spectre. *Educational Researcher, 16*(6), 19–21.

Takanishi, R. (1977). Federal involvement in early education (1933–1973): The need for historical perspectives. In L. G. Katz (Ed.), *Current topics in early childhood education* (Vol. 1, pp. 139–163). Norwood, NJ: Ablex Publishing Corporation.

Tobin, J. J. (1992). Early childhood education and the public schools: Obstacles to reconstructing a relationship. *Early Education and Development, 3*(2), 196–200.

Tout, K. (2013). Look to the stars: Future directions for the evaluation of Quality Rating and Improvement Systems. *Early Education and Development, 24*, 71–78.

Tucker, M. S. (2011, May). *Standing on the shoulders of giants: An American agenda for education reform.* Washington, DC: National Center on Education and the Economy.

Ubels, J., Fowler, A., & Acquaye-Baddoo, N-A. (2010). A resource volume on capacity development. In J. Ubels, N-A. Acquaye-Baddoo, & A. Fowler (Eds.), *Capacity development in practice* (pp. 1–8). London: Earthscan Ltd.

Urban, M. (2010). Rethinking professionalism in early childhood: Untested feasibilities and critical ecologies. *Contemporary Issues in Early Childhood, 11*(1), 1–7.

U.S. Department of Education & U.S. Department of Health and Human Services. (2011, August). *Race to the Top–Early Learning Challenge Executive Summary.* Washington, DC: Authors.

VanderVen, K. (1988). Pathways to professional effectiveness for early childhood education. In B. Spodek, O. N. Saracho, & D. L. Peters (Eds.), *Professionalism and the early childhood practitioner* (pp. 137–160). New York: Teachers College Press.

VanderVen, K. (1994). Professional development: A contextual model. In J. Johnson & J. B. McCracken (Eds.), *The early childhood career lattice: Perspectives on professional development* (pp. 79–88). Washington, DC: National Association for the Education of Young Children.

Weber, E. (1969). *The kindergarten: Its encounter with educational thought in America.* New York: Teachers College Press.

Wheatley, M. (1992). *Leadership and the new science.* San Francisco: Berrett-Koehler.

White, S. H., & Buka, S. L. (1987). Early education: Programs, traditions, and policies. In E. Z. Rothkopf (Ed.), *Review of research in education* (Vol. 14, pp. 43–97). Washington, DC: American Educational Research Association.

Whitebook, M. (2003). *Early education quality: Higher teacher qualifications for better learning environments—A review of the literature.* Berkeley, CA: Center for the Study of Child Care Employment, Institute for Research on Labor and Employment, University of California at Berkeley.

Whitebook, M. (2010, April). *No single ingredient: 2020 vision for the early learning workforce.* Presentation at the U.S. Department of Education and Health and Human Services Listening and Early Learning Tour on Workforce and Professional Development, Denver, CO. Available at http://www.ed_gov/about/initsled/earlylearning/denver-whitebook-speech.pdf

Whitebook, M., Austin, L. J. E., Ryan, S., Kipnis, F., Almaraz, M., & Sakai, L. (2012). *By default or by design? Variations in higher education programs for early care and education and their implications for research methodology, policy, and practice.* Berkeley, CA: Center for the Study of Child Care Employment, University of California, Berkeley.

Whitebook, M., & Ryan, S. (2011, April). Degrees in context: Asking the right questions about preparing skilled and effective teachers of young children. (Preschool Policy Brief No. 22). A joint publication of the National Institute for Early Education Research and the Center for the Study of Child Care Employment.

Willer, B., & Bredekamp, S. (1993). A "new" paradigm of early childhood professional development. *Young Children, 48*(4), 63–66.

Williams, B. (2011). All methods are wrong. Some methods are useful. *Systems Thinker, 22*(4), 4–7.

Williams, C. L. (1995). *Still a man's world: Men who do "women's work."* London: University of California Press.

Zellman, G. L., & Karoly, Y. (2012). *Approaches to incorporating child assessments into early childhood Quality Rating and Improvement Systems.* Santa Monica: CA: The RAND Corporation.

Zero to Three. (n.d.). *The future of infant-toddler child care.* Available at www. zerotothree.org/early-care-education-child-care/the-future-of-infant-toddlers.html

Zigler, E. (1999). Head Start is not child care. *American Psychologist, 54*(2), 142.

Zigler, E., Gilliam, W. S., & Barnett, W. S. (Eds.). (2011). *The pre-k debates: Current controversies & issues.* Baltimore: Paul H. Brookes.

Zigler, E., Marsland, K., & Lord, H. (2009). *The tragedy of child care in America.* New Haven, CT: Yale University Press.

Zivnuska, J. A. (1963). Forestry: A profession or a field of work? *Journal of Forestry, 61*(5), 339–340.

Zumwalt, K. K. (1984). Teachers and mothers: Facing new beginnings. *Teachers College Record, 86*(1), 138–155.

# Index

# About the Author and Contributors

*Stacie G. Goffin,* EdD is the principal of the Goffin Strategy Group. Established in 2004, the Goffin Strategy Group dedicates itself to building the ability of early childhood education to offer effective programs and services to young children through leadership and capacity- and systems-building. It works with state non-profits and governments, national organizations, and philanthropy. Stacie's conceptual leadership focuses on advancing early childhood education as a professional field of practice.

Prior to forming the Goffin Strategy Group, Stacie led the five-year effort to reinvent the National Association for the Education of Young Children's (NAEYC) early childhood program accreditation system. A former senior program officer at the Ewing Marion Kauffman Foundation, professor in higher education, and preschool educator, Stacie led the founding–and served as founding chair–of the Early Childhood Funders Collaborative, Kansas City's Metropolitan Council on Early Learning, and the West Virginia Network for Young Children. Goffin's publications are frequently recognized for their pioneering thinking.

**Rolf Grafwallner**, PhD is assistant state superintendent of the Division of Early Childhood Development at the Maryland State Department of Education. With a mission of improving early care and education quality and access for low-income children, focusing on children's successful transition into public school, the Division is responsible for state policy and technical support for all early childhood programs serving children, from birth through Kindergarten.

Dr. Grafwallner was instrumental in developing a statewide Kindergarten entry assessment, the first of its kind in the country. He helped develop policies for all-day Kindergarten and expanded the state's Pre-Kindergarten programs. He led efforts to consolidate early care and education programs into Maryland's department of education, creating a governance model for early childhood education nationally. He directed expansion of the Judy Center Partnerships, a statewide model of comprehensive public/private partnerships among public schools, early childhood, parenting, and health programs. Under his leadership, Maryland received a 2011 Race to the Top Early Learning Challenge Grant award.

**Jacqueline Jones**, PhD is the former deputy assistant secretary for Policy and Early Learning and senior advisor on Early Learning to the Secretary at the U.S. Department of Education. She has also served as assistant commissioner for the Division of Early Childhood Education in the New Jersey Department of Education.

Prior to state and federal government service, Dr. Jones worked for 15 years in the research division at Educational Testing Service in Princeton, New Jersey. She has given presentations across the country and has served on a number of national advisory committees including the Pew National Early Childhood Accountability Task Force and the National Research Council's Committee on Developmental Outcomes and Assessments for Young Children.

**Mary Jean Schumann, DNP, MBA, RN, CPNP, FAAN** is the interim senior associate dean of The George Washington University School of Nursing and the former executive director of the Nursing Alliance for Quality Care (NAQC). Schumann provides consultation on health strategies and issues relative to nursing and health care policy, advanced practice registered nurses (APRN), quality measurement, pediatric nursing, and pain management issues.

A fellow of the American Academy of Nursing, Schumann previously served at the American Nurses Association, first as director of nursing practice and policy, and more recently as chief programs officer. She served as the executive director of the National Pediatric Nurses Certification Board and the National Organization for Adolescent Pregnancy, Parenting, and Prevention.

**Pamela J. Winton**, PhD is a senior scientist and the director of outreach at FPG Child Development Institute. A prolific author and frequent member of advisory and review boards, Winton has been involved in research, outreach, technical assistance, professional development, and scholarly publishing related to early childhood for the last 3 decades. Winton is currently the director and principal investigator of two national technical assistance centers: the National Professional Development Center on Inclusion (NPDCI), whose purpose is to work with states to create a cross-agency system of high quality professional development (PD) for early childhood teachers; and CONNECT, bringing an evidence-based practice approach to professional development in key early childhood content areas. In 2002, she was awarded the Division of Early Childhood/Council for Exceptional Children's Service to the Field award.